To No
than
support during this
journey Jean François

Lasting Touch

*A Mother and Son's Journey Of Joy,
Challenges, Sadness and Discovery*

JEAN-FRANÇOIS PINSONNAULT

Tellwell Talent

www.tellwell.ca

ISBN

978-1-77302-405-9 (Hardcover)

978-1-77302-402-8 (Paperback)

978-1-77302-403-5 (eBook)

Table of Contents

To the memory of Lise and for everyone one out there who is considering taking care of one or both parents – it will be a memorable experience – even with the challenges that come with the journey.

Acknowledgments

Thank you to all my friends, Maureen, Lynn, Denise, Linda, Lisa, Jill and Janey who took the time to read and provide me with valuable ideas and suggestions. A special thank you to all my friends and colleagues who encouraged me in pursuing this labour of love.

Thank you Richard for being a good and faithful friend throughout my journey and for checking up on Mother so many times when I was away.

Thank you Françoise for listening patiently to my personal questioning and providing me with the confidence and comfort to pursue writing and publishing my memoirs about my wonderful journey with Mother as well as providing many great ideas.

Thank you to Norma Kennedy and Marc Bernier who edited the manuscript and provided me with great suggestions to make this book easier to read and understand.

Introduction

The phrase "Love one another" is so wise. By loving one another, we invest in each other and in ourselves. Perhaps someday, when we need someone to care for us, it may not come from the person we expect, but from the person we least expect. It may be our sons or daughters-in-law, our neighbors, friends, cousins, step-children, or stepparents whose love for us has assigned them to the honorable, yet dangerous position of caregiver.
— Peggi Speers, *The Inspired Caregiver: Finding Joy While Caring for Those You Love*

Lasting Touch is the true story of a mother and son's journey of joy, challenges, sadness, and discovery during their lives together as adults. Listening to his heart rather than to those who saw his decision to care for his elderly mother as unusual and unrealistic, Jean-François took every step possible to provide a comfortable environment for her in the home they shared for nearly four years prior to her passing away.

Through the good times and challenging times, he learned of the importance that an elderly parent puts on independence, dignity, respect, and comfort. This story reveals the tremendous lasting impact that the experience of being his mother's primary caregiver has had on Jean-François' life, and describes the insights he gained.

Although not everyone may be in a position to take care of an elderly parent, this book will give readers something to think about, along with some insights and available resources that can help ensure the wellness and safety of their loved ones.

Prologue

My family is described as a typical agricultural French-Canadian family of the era. My father, François, was born in 1908 of a medium-sized family of multi-purpose farmers located in the Eastern Townships of the province of Québec, about an hour south-east from Montréal. Like many farmers of the time, they worked the land to make a living and comfortably sustain their family. As the eldest, my father was sent to college, and then went to work for an uncle at the Port of Montréal.

My mother, Lise, born in 1912, was the youngest of a very large, middle-class family. Many of her older siblings were either stillborn or died during the flu epidemic of 1918.

My parents met at a community dance and it was love at first sight. They married in 1935. Over the following three years, Mother gave birth to three children—two girls, Josée and Andrée, and a boy, Michel. Mother tended house and raised the children while Father worked on the wharf, managing the loading and unloading of transport ships—a career he held for nearly 50 years.

In 1942, after a lengthy and difficult time, Michel died at age four of a form of cancer. Remaining in their house in Montreal was too painful to bear, so my parents moved with their two young daughters to the Eastern Townships where my father had been raised. There they rented and eventually bought an old farmhouse with substantial acreage.

Over the following seven years, with no electricity and few of the amenities and benefits of living in a big city, Mother gave birth to three boys—Antoine, Daniel, and me, Jean-François. As the youngest, I had been lucky enough to be born a few months after electricity was available in the farming community where we lived.

Due to the harshness of the area, the Second World War, the nearly impassable roads during the rainy season as well as the heavy snowfalls of the winter months, Josée and Andrée were enrolled at the convent in the nearby village where they stayed during the school year. Father paid their keep by providing wood for the convent's furnace.

Until the end of the war in 1945, Father was often called upon to go to Halifax, Nova Scotia, and supervise the loading of merchant ships bound for England while Mother cared for the children and managed the fledgling farm.

During the summer months, she grew vegetables, which she sold in exchange for hard-to-come-by items such as sugar and flour. Every member of the family had a role to play in ensuring there was food on the table. Whether it meant caring for the animals, growing and harvesting food, cutting wood up to a year in advance to heat the house and cook meals as soon as we were old enough to take on various responsibilities, then we all participated in one way or another.

Every time she went to the village during the school year, usually riding a horse or with a buggy, she went to see her two young daughters. Of course, the girls came home to the farm for the summer and other vacations—times they always enjoyed and obviously preferred.

Except for the winter months, Father spent weekdays and some weekends working on the wharf while Mother and the children took care of the daily activities with the help of a farmhand who worked for us Monday through Thursday.

As a child, I did my chores, went to school, and played outside. In my early teens I was bedridden for nearly two years with rheumatic fever, so Mother not only took care of me, but also managed the household, the farm and raised five children.

Over the years, all my siblings got married to raise their own families. On the other hand, I never married, choosing to focus on my education and my career. I was able to attend a local college, which allowed me to live at home and support Mother in managing the farm during Father's absence. When it was time to go to university, I chose the University of Ottawa to complete my Bachelor of Arts. Years later, I would go to McGill University in Montréal to do a masters.

I stayed relatively close to home until I was about 30 years old. At that time, in order to pursue my interests and my career, I moved to Montréal and eventually to the Ottawa region. This path probably contributed to my ability to care for my mother during the last years of her life.

Chapter 1
Mother's Failing Health

In 1980, a few years after retiring from his career on the wharf, my father passed away in his sleep from a heart attack. Although he had experienced various medical issues in previous years, there was a belief by the entire family that the worst was over. Father had been everything to Mother; they had been together for 45 years and suddenly he was gone. Her entire married life had been dedicated to her husband and her children. Now a very big part of her was gone.

During the weeks that followed my father's funeral, my siblings and I rallied around Mother, but it was still very difficult for her. Things got better as the months passed. Her will to live and the support of us children helped her to carry on. Though she spoke of Father often, reminiscing about the joys of their life together, we knew that inside she missed him terribly. She continued to be the rallying point for the entire family.

As December rolled in, I thought about how I might reduce the sadness of Mother's not being with her beloved husband during this special season. To provide a very different environment, I invited her to come with me to Florida for Christmas. For as long as I could remember, Christmas Day had been a family event, until my siblings one by one got married and went off to raise a family and spend Christmas with their children. In order to have a family gathering, they all came back to spend a few days around the 31st of December. This was the time for getting together, preparing meals, gift giving, and celebrating and wishing good tidings for the New Year.

She was hesitant about the proposed trip, but I talked about how she had wanted to go in the past but things had never worked out. I also said we could go to see one of her sisters-in-law who spent the winter on the west coast of Florida. Mother agreed to go, so I made all the arrangements to fly to Tampa. From there we drove to St. Petersburg where I had rented an apartment for a week. We had a grand time. We took long walks along the beach. Mother did have some difficulty adjusting to all the lights on palm trees and the fact that there was no snow. We also visited her sister-in-law while we were there and took in various sights of interest.

On Christmas Day, I cooked up a feast for two. I had become quite a good cook, thanks to the dedicated patience of Mother while I was growing up and my need to innovate and explore various flavours. For this special occasion, I prepared a Cornish hen stuffed with pecans and apricot jam, vegetables, scalloped potatoes, and for dessert, a cheesecake with fresh fruit on top.

As a reader, you might wonder why I took the liberty of including recipes in such a story. Food growing and preparation was for us a family affair. It was an opportunity to engage in communication and share in the various tasks.

Many of my memories of mother throughout my various stages of growing up involved preparing meals, enjoying the meal as a family and then cleaning-up. Even after the arrival of television, we sat around the table after the evening meal to talk about our individual day, share stories and even participate in some family games. When we needed help with our school homework, Mother, or Father when he was present, would help us with some of the harder parts.

Apricot Pecan Stuffed Cornish Hen
Makes two or three servings

A turkey, ham or any other roasting meat for two people is often too much and can also be costly unless you are intending to have guests over or plenty of leftovers. A Cornish hen is an option for providing an excellent source of protein, minimizing cost, and reducing leftovers. They are usually available in the frozen section of your grocery store. At certain times of the year you might even be able to find (or order) a fresh one.

Ingredients

1	Cornish hen (if frozen, thaw in refrigerator for 24 hours)
1	teaspoon of oil (e.g., olive, canola)

1	tablespoon of low-salt margarine or butter
¼	cup of bread cut in small cubes, or croutons
½	cup of chicken or vegetable low-salt broth (¼ cup for the stuffing and ¼ cup for pouring over Cornish hen in roaster)
¼	cup of chopped celery
1	small green onion chopped
1	medium mushroom, chopped (optional)
¼	cup of halved pecans
2	tablespoons of apricot no-sugar-added jam

Directions

1. Coat a small roasting pan with a teaspoon of oil. Put aside.

2. In a medium saucepan, cook celery, onion, and mushroom in margarine or butter until tender.

3. Add ¼ cup of broth and the bread cubes or croutons and stir until well blended. Simmer for 2-3 minutes. Remove from heat source.

4. Mix in pecans and apricot jam.

5. Stuff the mixture into the hen. Place in the roasting pan; pour the rest of the broth over the hen and cover.

6. Bake at 350° F for 75-80 minutes or until meat thermometer reads 165° F. Every 30 minutes or so, using a baster or ladle, take juices from the pan and pour over the hen.

7. Remove the cover of the roasting pan for the last 3-5 minutes of cooking for a browner and crispier skin.

Complement the Cornish hen with your favourite vegetables and potatoes or rice. If you are so inclined, a glass of your favourite dry white wine is a great accompaniment. Bon appétit!

Things went well for the next two years or so. Mother kept busy. During the summer months it was her flower gardens and a small vegetable patch. She visited and kept in touch with various friends and family members, travelling on occasion to visit those who were further away while we still got together for various holidays and family events. During the winter months she tended to stay at home as she did not enjoy driving long distances, only going to the village nearby for her weekly groceries. There is no doubt that she missed her beloved husband.

Then, Mother got very ill. The doctors concluded that she had experienced multiple strokes and that she needed lots of rest because she was extremely fragile. They were unsure if she would be able to walk again because she was so weak. She had to be hospitalized at the Montreal Neurological Institute for a few months. Mother was very weak and could not eat by herself.

Unfortunately, her stay at the hospital coincided with a strike by hospital staff. With the limited number of people working on each ward, it could not be guaranteed that someone would have the time to ensure she would actually be fed. Being the nearest of her children to the institute, I went to the hospital every day during meal times to feed her.

After weeks at the Neurological Centre, experiencing test after test and enduring the strike by hospital workers, Mother's strength improved. Eventually, I was able to get the doctors to agree to let her go home on the condition we get a qualified caregiver to stay with her.

I called my siblings and friends to get the message out that I was looking for a live-in person to take care of

Mother in her own home. I did get a bit of resistance as some of my siblings wanted to put Mother in a care facility. However, mother felt very strongly that being in her own house would be best for her as long as we could get someone to live with her and provide the care she needed until she was able to get her strength back.

Within a few weeks Mother was moved back to the farm. It took some time before we found the right caregiver. Eventually, we found a qualified caregiver who had her own car, wanted to live in the country, and most of all hit it off with Mother. With the care and dedication of Denise, Mother regained much of her strength, though never to the level she had before.

While Mother did improve tremendously, the previous ten years had not been without its challenges. Open sores on her legs were a source of constant pain and required daily care. Her eyesight had diminished to the point where she was considered legally blind—her vision only allowed her to see as if she were looking through a drinking straw. (Try it sometime; you will experience firsthand the significant limitations.)

From the time that Mother's health declined in 1982, I drove down to Cowansville every other week to spend weekends with her. This would give her companion Denise some time off. I would bring all sorts of food items and I would prepare different dishes. Mother and I would spend hours talking.

After a couple of years, I invited my sisters and brothers to a meeting to ask them for some help. Although they were agreeable, their help did not materialize in a consistent manner, which was disappointing. However,

I did not let their behaviour deter me as I continued to spend time with Mother every two weeks. One of my visits would be for the entire weekend and the other for a day.

For nearly ten years, Mother lived in her home on the farm with her companion. Denise took care of her by being a friend and supporting Mother in her daily needs. We would often call each other to talk about various things. The brothers and sisters who lived in the area would visit from time to time or call. At different times, we would all go over, usually for special events or holidays; we would prepare meals and enjoy each other's company.

Though her strength had improved, over time her already limited eyesight diminished significantly and the occasional sores on her legs seemed to have become permanent. They required regular attention and greatly reduced her mobility. She took a variety of medication to prevent new strokes. I would often ask her to come and live with me, but she would refuse, saying that this was her home and she was not ready to leave.

Mother's illness had made her very fragile. Because the sores on her legs had worsened, she struggled to go up and down the stairs to her bedroom. We finally convinced her that it would be safer if she slept downstairs. The family room was transformed into a bedroom. We all felt better knowing that she did not have to tackle the staircase. Denise had her quarters upstairs, which gave her privacy. Now and then, Mother would go up with Denise. They would walk around together from room to room. She would talk about the different events that took place in each nook and cranny.

She enjoyed being downstairs; however, she would sometimes comment that if she had the strength, she would brighten up the room.

One weekend when I was there, Denise told me about Mother's comments and said that she would gladly do the painting. We talked it over and Mother was delighted at the prospect. We got out the Sears catalogue and started looking for ideas. Mother had shopped by catalogue for years, so we quickly found what she wanted. Over the following weeks everything was done. She had a newly decorated bedroom with matching curtains and bedspread: roses on an off-white background, a green carpet, and white furniture. This minor change meant the world to Mother.

Chapter 2
Beginning a Major
Life Change

The 1989-1990 recession, coupled with the sale of a small café I had co-owned with a business partner, forced me to look for alternative employment. As a self-employed consultant, I had worked with a number of large and medium-size businesses in the Montréal area to improve their organizational efficiency and performance. With the downturn in the economy, the first to get hit were the external consultants such as myself. In all fairness, most of my client companies were extremely accommodating and gave me about six months advance warning.

I brushed up my résumé and began a job search. I tapped into my network of colleagues and scanned the papers for career opportunities. Several of the ads resulted in interviews. One in particular, a research facility in the

Ottawa Valley, was in need of someone with my skills in the area of organizational development. Following the interviews, they made me an offer.

I took a few days to reflect on this potential major change in my life. I was 40 years old at the time. I had never envisioned that I would leave my family and friends and move away to another region, never mind another province to further my career. It was a big decision, yet my intuition about the whole prospect was positive, so I accepted. I would now be moving to the Ottawa Valley, an environmentally pristine rural area surrounded by extensive forests, hills, small lakes, and a variety of wildlife.

I sublet a small one-bedroom, sparsely-furnished apartment in the neighbouring town of Pembroke. It wasn't long before I discovered why the previous tenant had vacated. Unbeknownst to me, the apartment adjoined the back wall of a squash court. The repetitive thumping sounds of squash balls hitting my living room wall became regular evening competition to the television and radio. It wasn't long before I seriously considered breaking my lease—a costly alternative to the earplugs I had purchased.

As the months went by, I settled into my routine, getting to know more about the area and my job and colleagues. That first winter was so bitterly cold that it was not unusual to find the tires of my car frozen as I made my way to work at seven in the morning. I was thankful that my parking space included an outlet to plug in my block heater overnight, so I could get the car started and reach that first kilometre where the squared tires would begin to round themselves out. Never had I experienced such cold nights. The bonus was that the extreme cold kept people away from the fitness centre, affording me some relatively quiet evenings.

On weekends I would drive to Terrasse-Vaudreuil on Île Perrot, a small island on the western tip of Montréal, where I had purchased a house some years earlier. Most weekends were spent fixing or painting in the house in preparation for putting it up for sale except on weekends when I visited Mother.

About two months before the end of my lease, I started looking for another apartment. At first I went through the paper and the bulletin board at the grocery store to see what I could find but to no avail. One day while at work, I was describing my predicament to my colleagues and one of them told me she had a friend who owned a small bed and breakfast about twenty minutes from our workplace, on a country road on the west side of Pembroke.

She immediately got on the phone and, after a brief conversation, she arranged for us to meet the following Saturday morning to see what kind of living arrangements could be made. The house was situated at the end of a long laneway, very close to the main highway I took to go to work. A few mature trees and several old buildings, that in the past had likely served as a thriving farm, surrounded it.

Upon our arrival, a lady in her late sixties or early seventies came out the side door. My friend introduced me to Bea. After exchanging a few words, she invited us to go in for a tour of the house. We entered the house through the wood shed, which was typical for a farmhouse. As we walked into the kitchen, it was obvious that this was the main room of the house; it represented about half of the ground floor. To one side was an old-style double sink with a window facing the barnyard. On the adjoining side were a wood stove and an electric range. There were a few cupboards, a large table and four chairs in the centre of the room, along with various solid wood pieces of furniture. A staircase went up to Bea's quarters on the second floor—an area of the house I never saw.

The small living room was furnished with various antique pieces of furniture and a great many plants. An old-style pedestal sink, a toilet, and a vintage clawfoot bathtub shared the bathroom. Adjoining it was a parlour and another staircase that went up to two small bedrooms. Both were furnished with a dresser, a rod-iron double bed, a chair, and a lamp. The whole house was very clean and fresh-smelling. However, I felt like I had stepped back in time to the 1940s or 1950s.

Bea was a delightfully witty and energetic lady. We sat in the parlour and chatted over a cup of tea and some homemade cookies. We quickly hit it off. After discussing the financial aspect, we made plans for me to move in within the following couple of weeks. The transfer was quick as I had very few things to take—a comfortable chair I had purchased after my initial move, a reading lamp, and my clothes. I was coming to live here temporarily in this quaint and comfortable country home until I could find more permanent accommodations.

Over the following months, Bea and I became great friends. She had given me the best room in the house and I felt quite at home. Though I was in a country B&B,

it felt like I was part of her family as I had the run of most of the house.

On weekends I drove to Terrasse-Vaudreuil or to Cowansville, usually coming back late Sunday evening. During weekend trips, I took the opportunity to do my laundry either at home or at Mother's.

Weekdays, Bea made me breakfast before I headed to work. In the evening, we had dinner together and we would spend hours talking about her life experiences. Both of us had loved ones who were far away, so sharing our experiences, our joys, and our sadness was comforting. We enjoyed each other's company. Bea was like a second mother to me.

Bea would often call me at work in the afternoon to ask if I had plans for dinner. When I did not, which was most of the time, she would invite me to have dinner with her after work. My many offers to compensate her for the excellent cooking were always refused. "It gives me a purpose to eat better," she would add.

Wanting to compensate for her generosity, I helped out around the house as much as possible by doing the dishes, making my bed every morning, bringing wood from the shed into the kitchen, and every now and then buying groceries. In the winter I would remove the snow from the steps and tackle the odd jobs she needed done.

In return, she showed her appreciation by having a shower enclosure installed around the bathtub while I was away one weekend. She decided on her own that it would be more convenient for me to take a shower instead of a bath every morning before going to work. She had guessed right!

Though I offered to clean and vacuum my room, she insisted that she clean the house from top to bottom once a week, that it was good exercise. I had been living with Bea for several months when my house in Terrasse-Vaudreuil sold and put my belongings in storage. Bea and I had a good arrangement, so I had no plans to move on.

One Friday morning in early December while we were having breakfast, I asked her if she decorated for Christmas. She indicated that she used to, but in the past few years she had found it too difficult. I offered to stay the following weekend and decorate. I drove to Terrasse-Vaudreuil for the weekend as usual and returned on Sunday after dinner.

As I drove into the yard, I noticed there was a good-sized fir tree leaning against the shed. After coming in and saying hello, I went up to put my things in my room before joining Bea for a cup of tea and catching up on the weekend events.

When I asked her where she had bought the tree, I was caught off-guard, given she was in her seventies. She had gone into the forest behind her house, cut down a tree and brought it back to the house on her own. She was looking forward to decorating it and hoped to start during the week. On Monday evening it stood, small chunks of ice melting, branches stretching, and transformed into a beautiful cone shape for decorating.

Over the next couple of days, we hung several strands of lights and many beautiful antique ornaments Bea had brought down from her attic. By mid-week, we had a beautiful Christmas tree that we could enjoy when we sat in the parlour to watch television. Outside, I used some colourful shiny red paper and white ribbon and turned the front door—which was not used during the winter—into what looked like a very large wrapped gift, complete with some pine branches and a few lights. One evening after dinner, we put our boots and coats on and went for a walk down the lane, so we could see the gift-wrapped door and the tree lit up in the parlour. The idea to gift-wrap the door came from my mother who had wrapped the front door back on the farm each Christmas. Bea was absolutely delighted with the result.

The weekend before Christmas, I went to see Mother and did all the decorations. In the house I decorated a small table tree and placed some other ornaments in the rest of the house. Outside on the snow covered lawn, I decorated one of the tall fir trees with green and blue lights, which were Mother's favourite colours. To this day, I still decorate one of the outside trees with blue and green lights, in memory of Mother.

Everything would be ready for my return trip at Christmas. My employer arranged for most of us to have the Christmas week with our families. Spending that time with Mother was always very special. Some of my siblings and their families would drop by on Christmas Day. On or around New Year's Day, I either prepared a meal for the whole family or everyone would bring a dish and we celebrated the New Year together.

After a particularly cold and harsh winter, the first signs of spring were beginning to show. The blanket of snow, which covered the fields and mountain peaks for many months, was slowly being pulled away like the heavy woollen blankets of our beds.

The chatter around the bird feeders was noticeably increasing. The winter regulars of chickadees, blue jays, cardinals, grosbeaks, and mourning doves were now being challenged by various other species to get their share of the daily meal. Bea had been out filling all the feeders with all sorts of seeds. As long as she stood there, the regulars would come to perch and eat as they knew her so well. The others would sit in the nearby trees and chatter, hoping she would be scared away. She would leave only when she knew that her winter friends had gotten first choice. There was plenty for all yet she had her favourites. This daily routine was part of her life and now part of mine as well.

On this particular weekend in late April, I had stayed in Pembroke simply to relax. I no longer had to drive to Terrasse-Vaudreuil as I had sold the house in the fall. The driving back and forth had been taking its toll as I had been doing this for nearly two years. It was now time to take a break from driving and enjoy the weekend.

It was a beautiful sunny and mild Saturday morning. I decided to go sit on the porch steps to finish my coffee after breakfast. The sun warmed my face. I stared at the old buildings of what was probably a busy barnyard in years past. They had become the hunting grounds for Chinny, Bea's faithful cat. He was on the prowl. I could hear in the background the many sounds of birds singing the arrival of spring. My mind was wandering.

I had come to this place to further my career, leaving behind friends and family.

At first it had been difficult, but now I enjoyed the country environment; after all, I had been born and raised on a farm, so it certainly was not foreign to me. However, having lived in a large city environment for many years prior, coming back to the country had also brought its challenges.

At that very moment I did not know that minutes later my life would change in such a way that I could never have imagined.

Chapter 3
Is the Offer Still Good?

"François," called Bea, "your mother is on the phone." I was startled by Bea's voice. Though she had addressed me by that name since the first day we had met, it often caught me off guard as François was also my father's name. My friends and colleagues called me Jean or Jean-François.

Although it was not unusual for Mother to phone me, when she did it was usually in the evening after dinner. I wondered if there was anything wrong. I quickly made my way to the phone. "Allo maman, comment ça va? Is everything all right?"

"Yes", she answered. "Everything is fine. How are you doing? How is your work?"

We exchanged a few words, catching up on each other's latest events. Then out of the blue she said, "I want to ask you something."

"Sure, Mother. What is it?"

"Well, last weekend when you were down to see me, I wanted to talk about different things, but I was not able to do so."

"What is it, Mother?" I asked.

"Well, winter was very harsh. It is very difficult to keep this big old house warm.

Your brother tries to come over regularly to put some big pieces of wood in the furnace, but he is so busy with the sugar bush and everything that the fire often dies out and I have to use the electric baseboard system, which really is not much help. If I stay in the kitchen it is not too bad with the stove burning full blast, but as soon as I leave that room it gets very cold. It was like that all winter and I do not think I want to do that another winter."

For the past ten years or so, you have asked me to come and live with you and I have refused. After this past winter, however, I think I am ready to leave. I am going to be 80 this year and I think it is time for me to live in a more comfortable environment.

So, I was thinking, is your offer still good? Can I come and live with you? Please feel free to say no. I do understand that you have your own life and taking care of me is probably not in your plans right now."

I paused for a few seconds. It was true that I had offered many times, but she had always said no. What would this mean? Was I able to care for her? Where would we live?

For several years, my focus had been on keeping my skills and education current while pursuing my career aspirations, maintaining contact with my colleagues and friends, and travelling both for business or pleasure. During my adult years, I practiced various summer sports (cycling, hiking, and swimming) and during the winter I mostly did alpine skiing. I had travelled across Canada several times, been to Europe and North Africa, to Australia as well as many interesting places in the United States. With no real attachment, I could, with very little notice, pack a bag and leave on a business trip or vacation.

Would I be able to handle this major change in my life-style? Many questions bombarded my mind. Regardless, I knew that things would all fall into place eventually. Then as quickly as these thoughts had gone through my mind I responded.

"Certainement, maman. When would you like to move in with me?" I said.

"Are you sure?" she said. "This is a big decision."

"Yes, I know. However, I do want you to come and live with me. I will make some arrangements and get things organized, so you can move in as soon as possible."

"No, no," she said. "I was actually thinking about some time in the fall. I would like to spend the summer here at the farm. It's so beautiful during the summer with the trees and flowers. I always enjoy sitting outside on the veranda. Also, Denise is willing to stay with me until the fall."

I was actually quite pleased that she wanted to spend the summer in her home as this would give me ample time to explore various options to determine where exactly we would settle down. Determining where we would live was one of the many issues I had to think through.

There was also the need to identify all the various support systems for Mother and, depending on where we chose to live, the possibility of having to find a job nearby. And last but certainly not least, was the task of letting the rest of the family know about Mother's decision.

Throughout my teenage years and much of my adult life, I had often felt discounted or ignored by my father and siblings. As I was the baby of the family, they seemed to think that I was not likely to have good ideas or be responsible. My father had long treated me as the weak one—the one who had been sick and could not contribute in the same fashion as my older brothers and sisters.

Over time, I developed some sort of shield against their attitude and behaviour, but it lingered at the back of my mind. As I grew older, I compensated by being the best at what I did, mostly trying to do things all by myself, to show that I was capable, that I could and did contribute.

So, letting my sisters and brothers know about Mother's upcoming living arrangements would certainly be difficult for one or two of them to accept. However, the fact still remained, this was Mother's decision, which she had pondered for many years and I was in total acceptance.

"Mother, have you spoken to the others about your decision yet?"

"No, first I wanted to make sure you still wanted me to come and live with you."

"I am sure they won't be very surprised; however, you should tell them."

"Yes, you're right. I'll call them."

Then an idea came to me. "Non, attends. J'ai une idée. Why don't I organize a get-together for Mother's Day? It is a few weeks away. I will call everyone and invite them to your house for a Sunday brunch. We do this every year, so it won't come as a surprise to anyone. I'll come in on the Saturday and prepare everything. How does that sound? Is it okay with you?"

"Yes, it sounds like a great idea," she replied.

"Good! I'll call all of them and invite them."

We said our goodbyes and I spent the rest of the weekend making plans and calling everyone.

On the Saturday morning of Mother's Day weekend, I drove to Cowansville. I spent the day cooking and baking some of the dishes that could be done in advance. I made sure to make my famous "bagatelle," or trifle, that my nieces and nephews always appreciated. I wanted to make sure that there would be plenty to eat as my siblings and their families had good appetites.

Bagatelle (Trifle) de Jean-François

During the years I worked as a management consultant, I also co-owned a small café. In the evening, I did all the cooking for the next day, including baking the muffins, croissants, cakes, and pies as well as the lunch specials. I developed a number of recipes that were easy and quick to make. After several tests, we knew what our patrons enjoyed most, so we accommodated them.

Among these items were my four-tier cakes. One dessert that I made on a regular basis is a "bagatelle" or trifle. It was something I put together once and, due to its popularity, ended up making weekly. After moving to Pembroke, my new employer, as a policy, stated that all new employees were to undergo a complete physical. It was at that time that I discovered I had diabetes, so from then on when I cooked I replace sugars with sweeteners.

Ingredients

1	single-layer homemade or store-bought pound cake (vanilla, chocolate, or marble) cut into one-inch cubes
4	cups (2 small boxes – 10-11 gr) of no-sugar-added jelly powder (cherry, raspberry, strawberry, or lemon)
1	can (540 ml) of no-sugar-added fruit salad, drained, or fresh fruit of your choice
2	cups (1 box) of no-sugar-added instant pudding (vanilla, strawberry, or white chocolate)

Enough whipped cream to top each serving.

Directions

1. *Prepare jelly powder according to directions and set aside.*
2. *Put the cut-up cake cubes in your serving bowl. A clear glass bowl provides a great visual.*
3. *Spread the drained fruit salad or an equivalent amount of fresh fruit evenly over the cake.*
4. *Pour the prepared jelly powder over the cake and fruit and place in the refrigerator until set.*
5. *Once the jelly has set, prepare the instant pudding and spread evenly over the mixture. Refrigerate.*
6. *When ready, add a dollop of whipped cream on top and serve.*

Variation: For a Black Forest trifle, use chocolate cake, cherry jelly powder, chocolate chips and/or maraschino cherries instead of fruit salad, and top with either dark chocolate or white chocolate instant pudding.

During the brunch, Mother talked about how the past winter had been very difficult for her and that she had made a decision to go and live somewhere else. The sudden silence by everyone in the room was eerie. Everyone looked at Mother somewhat surprised. Finally, one of my siblings said, "Qu'est-ce que tu as dit, maman?"

"J'ai dit que j'avais décidé d'aller vivre ailleurs," Mother announced.

"But where are you going to live?" asked one of my brothers.

"Well, I have been thinking about this for a few months now and after talking it over with him, I have agreed to go live with Jean-François. He has been inviting me to come and live with him since your father passed away, but I was not ready. Now I am."

There was another pause. My sister Josée spoke up. "I think this is great. I have been unwell for a while now and I often think of you in this big house. I wish we could do something, but John has his hands full with me right now."

Josée had been diagnosed with breast cancer. The discovery of the disease had come very late in the progression. She had been receiving chemotherapy, but the side effects made her extremely ill. Over time, her condition had deteriorated and she had had a stroke, which paralyzed one side of her body. Eventually we all realized that her time with us was limited, but we decided not to emphasize that fact to Mother until the inevitable. We all knew that it would be very hard for Mother, having already lost to illness her first son and her beloved husband as well as all her brothers and sisters in years prior.

For the rest of the meal as well as throughout the afternoon, the conversation centred around the move, where we would live, when Mother would be moving, and so on. I explained to everyone that I had a very good lead for a job in Ottawa, and if everything went as planned I would buy a house in the Ottawa area and Mother would move at the end of October. I could sense that there were some concerns not being spoken. By late afternoon everyone had gone home, after saying his or her goodbyes. I left to return to Pembroke.

Throughout the entire trip, my mind went through all the events of the past several weeks. It was done. Mother and I would be living together by the time the leaves had changed colour. This was going to be a change for me and for her. Would I regret this decision? Time would tell. However, I had a good feeling about my decision.

"To care for those who once cared for us is one of the highest honors." — Tia Walker, *The Inspired Caregiver: Finding Joy While Caring for Those You Love*

Chapter 4
Finding the Right
Place to Live

Several weeks had passed since the big announcement. I had started to look at all my options. I could stay in my present job, buy a house and live in the Pembroke area, or I could move to Ottawa. I had been offered a job there several months earlier but had turned it down as I enjoyed the different challenges and experiences provided to me by my current job in the valley. I loved my job and my new friends and colleagues, so I saw no need to move again. It had taken me many months to get used to my new environment. Leaving Montreal to come to the Pembroke area had been difficult, but now I liked the region.

However, change was in the air. My organization was downsizing and my position might be in jeopardy; therefore, it was time to explore other opportunities.

A quick review of the different support systems and resources available for the elderly pointed to Ottawa. So I decided to check out job opportunities there. I would start with the one that had been offered to me several months prior. I called my contact there.

"Hello, Rosemary! This is Jean-François. How have you been?"

"Great, and you?" she replied.

"Very well, thanks. Rosemary, I have a question for you."

"Sure," she said. "What is it?"

"The last time we spoke you indicated that you would like me to join your organization. At that time, I had to decline. Well, there have been a few changes in my life and I was wondering if the position is still vacant."

"What has changed your mind?" she asked.

"Do you remember when we spoke, I told you about my mom and how I was trying to get her to move in with me? Well, she should be arriving in the fall. I have done some research and have discovered that the Ottawa region has many resources and support systems for the elderly. So, I would like to know more about the position you offered me, if it is still open."

Rosemary replied, "As a matter of fact, I am glad you called. Not only have I not been able to fill the position, but also it has become imperative for the organization that we get a qualified resource. Can you come in this week?"

Two days later, I sat in the Director General's office, talking about my qualifications and my experience. I noticed that the more I talked, the more the two of them glanced at each other and I could see what were almost undetectable smiles. In my mind I wondered if I was saying the things they wanted to hear, or worse, that I was totally off track. This went on for nearly two hours. They asked me several questions. They described in detail a number of "for instance" situations and asked me how I would deal with each one. After what seemed like an eternity, Rosemary noticed that it was past noon.

"Let's go eat and we can talk some more about what we are facing and what we would expect from you," she said. Pleased, I realized that I had impressed them.

After ordering lunch, we chatted about my mother— what had brought her to change her mind and how I was dealing with it all. I could tell that both had some interest in what I was about to undertake. The conversation eventually moved on to the topic of the position and what it entailed.

They gave me historical background on this major government department, an overview of the anticipated changes planned for the future, the different initiatives attempted in the past, and the mixed results achieved. They spoke of the support they knew they could get from some of the senior managers as well as some of the barriers that would be encountered along the way.

The challenge was certainly appealing—to set up an Organizational Development group that would help the organization to effectively manage the major change initiatives planned for the next few years. I was excited by the possibilities.

They informed me that the job was going to be re-posted and that I should apply. They were confident that I was a good candidate and that I would be successful because the previous posting had not yielded any suitable candidates. They were very forthright and direct. They could only guarantee a two-year contract, after which the position would have to be reviewed. I now realized that the faint smiles I had observed earlier signified that I was the qualified resource they had been searching for. The different experiences I had talked about earlier were very similar to what they were describing. They highlighted the different processes involved. My skills and abilities would have to be formally tested in order to meet the profile of the position. We hashed out the final details and timelines.

Within a few weeks I had made some of the biggest decisions of my life. One major issue remained—where Mother and I would live. That night I called my sister Andrée. She had lived in the Ottawa region for several years and could probably give me some ideas of where I could find a house that would meet Mother's needs as well as my own.

Andrée and I talked for a while. She invited me to come down on the weekend and we would look at different options. I arrived late-morning Saturday. Andrée was out getting groceries but David, her husband, was there, mowing the lawn. We sat outside and talked about Mother moving in with me. I could sense that he was trying subtly to change my mind, but my decision was made. There was no turning back.

My sister arrived from shopping. I helped her put things away and then we had a quick lunch. The conversation centered on me and Mother. Was I ready for such a change in lifestyle? How would I manage taking care of an elderly blind woman? Did I fully understand the extent of my decision? To this day I remember the questioning; however, I also remember that I kept my cool, as I knew I was doing the right thing.

I explained to both of them that I had two reasons for making my decision. First, Mother needed me; she could no longer live on the farm and she was too far away for me to really help out. The other siblings who were closer were not in a position to help very much due to their own commitments. If Mother lived with me, I could ensure her well-being and comfort. Besides, if we insisted on putting her into a retirement home, she would be very unhappy and would undoubtedly lose her will to live, which was not acceptable to me. I had been offering Mother to come and live with me for ten years and now she was ready and she had accepted my offer.

As for my second reason, all my siblings were aware. In my youth, I had been very ill for nearly two years with rheumatic fever and Mother had taken care of me during that time. Now it was time for me to give her the same consideration. Though I was the youngest of the family, I could do this and I was determined to take on this responsibility.

When the question "Where are you going to live?" came, I was ready. "Somewhere in the Ottawa region."

"But what about your job? Are you going to commute?"

"No," I said. "I have several options here in town. If everything goes as planned, I should be starting a new job at the beginning of August."

They were stunned. After I gave them some of the details, they seemed to let up on the questioning.

The rest of the day was uneventful, capped with a delightful dinner, a quiet evening, and a good night's sleep. The next morning at breakfast, I was surprised by an unforeseen invitation. If I wanted, I could come and stay with Andrée and David for a few weeks once I started my new job, until I found a house in the area. I was overcome with joy.

Later that day, my brother Antoine called. After a brief conversation, he suggested that we organize a party for Mother's eightieth birthday at the end of June. He also asked if Andrée would mind having it at her place; that way we could include all of Mother's relatives (many of whom lived in the area) and let everyone know about Mother's move to the Ottawa region.

Mother's birthday party was a success. It was a total surprise for her. Though her sisters and brothers had all passed away, many of their children had families of their own and lived in the region. It was a beautiful sunny day and everyone had a great time. At the appropriate time, I announced to all present that Mother would be moving in with me in the region in the fall. The general response was, "Ma tante, Lise, c'est formidable." All of my cousins had spent many summers and winters on the farm with tante Lise and oncle François. Our proximity now would make it easier for them to visit.

The formal staffing process for my new work position took its course and, though demanding, went well. By mid-July I was confirmed in the new job and I would start the second week of August.

After giving my official resignation at my current job, I completed all my files or transferred what could not be completed to my colleagues. I said my goodbyes to all my friends and colleagues. Leaving Bea was especially difficult. We had become very good friends and she was truly a great lady. I promised I would come and see her and I would write. I put the few things I had brought with me in the same storage facility I had used when I had moved from Montreal. I packed my clothes and moved into my sister's basement.

After settling in to my new job in Ottawa, I began the search for a house. After due consideration and regular conversations with Mother, we decided that our house should be situated outside of Ottawa, somewhere in the countryside. Mother had lived for 50 years on a farm. The nearest neighbour had been over a kilometre away (almost a mile). I certainly could not bring Mother to live in the middle of the city. We both loved having gardens. However, Mother was not very stable on her feet because of her legs and her eyesight was very limited. We needed to have a deck that was large enough for her to sit comfortably and securely outside. Ideally, I would have my own quarters or living area. Though we were going to live with each other, I had come to realize—through my inquiries and my research—that we both would need some privacy.

I met with a representative from Home Care Services to get more information on what was available and what I needed to know when it came to caring for an elderly parent. They were surprised and even somewhat sceptical to see that a male child was going to be the caregiver, and they were not shy about expressing their concerns, going as far as to question my real intentions for taking care of my mother.

From their point of view and experience, when children took care of their aging parents, it had been either the daughter or the daughter-in-law who had taken on this responsibility. Having the son take on this role was unusual in their eyes. Regardless, the meetings with various sources were extremely useful.

A very good friend from my previous employment had been very helpful in preparing me, given her past experiences. She gave me excellent ideas and suggestions. Most importantly, I had learned from her that for the months and years to come I should always endeavour to ensure that Mother retained as much control over her life as possible. Independence and autonomy were key to her comfort. This would also lessen my role in decision-making, as she would be involved in the discussions and final decisions, as she had been since this journey had begun in April.

However, years later I would discover that there was much more information and support available than I had actually discovered, such as the Canada Mortgage and Housing Corporation (CMHC). This federal Crown Corporation publishes countless publications, research papers, reports, and general information, and even provides some support to Canada's aging population through the different provinces.

The house-hunting experience—which I had figured would be a relatively easy task—painfully reminded me that some real estate agents sometimes do not totally listen to the needs of their clients. Prior to looking for a house, Mother and I had talked about her expectations and needs. Following these conversations, I had then spent several hours with an agent, explaining in detail what I was looking for in a house, such as the type of heating, availability of natural lighting, size of common areas, number of bedrooms, main living area on one floor with no or few steps due to Mother's limited eyesight, a large outside patio or deck, and a reasonably-sized lot located in a country setting.

He called back a few days later with a list of options. We went to visit the potential houses he had found for me, all to no avail. They were either in the city itself, had no land to speak of, sunken living rooms, bedrooms and living area on different floors, baseboard heating—all the things I had specifically said I did not want because of Mom's needs and limitations. After a few weeks of this, I decided to do some searching on my own and picked up different real estate flyers found in shopping malls and started going through them one by one. I found about a half dozen that seemed to meet my needs, at least from the written descriptions. I called the agent to set up a viewing schedule for the coming Saturday. He hesitated a bit but agreed.

He picked me up early Saturday morning and off we went to find the ideal home. The first few houses we saw were not bad; however, they required more renovations than I was prepared to do at this stage. We arrived at the third house on my list. The owners were away, but the agent had made arrangements for the keys. We entered via the front of the house, which led to an L-shaped room. The larger area was a living room with a fireplace. The smaller area was a fair-sized dining room with access to a patio door that led to a deck. A small yet efficient kitchen, three bedrooms, and a full bathroom completed the main floor.

As we made our way down to the lower level, there was a ground level back door, then a few more steps to the basement that opened up into a very large family room complete with a woodstove in the corner, another bedroom, a full bathroom, a laundry room, and a utility room. This was looking really good. No major repairs or renovations were required. It was in move-in condition.

We went back upstairs and went out back on to what turned out to be a large deck.

"Wow, this is absolutely wonderful," I said as I stood on the back deck looking toward what seemed like an acre of paradise.

"Is everything okay Jean-François?" asked the agent.

"Yes, why?"

"Well, what I see is several piles of rocks, dirt, and weeds."

"Yes, I see those as well, but I can see beyond all that. I see the potential it has. I can envision flower gardens along that side down to the back, some apple trees and maybe a gazebo over there in the corner, a small vegetable garden over here, and some bird feeders and a birdbath over here."

I had found our future home. Everything Mother would need was on the main floor. The rooms were fairly large and most of her furniture would look great. And, last but not least, a beautiful backyard with a huge deck. The basement would be ideal for my quarters, privacy yet proximity, all this within twenty minutes of the city core.

We continued the tour to see the other houses. They all had charm yet by the end of the day my mind was made up. I would put an offer on the third house we had visited. The agent suggested we wait a day or two since there was already an offer from another buyer. I did not want to lose that house. I was not in a mood for getting into a bidding war. I wanted that house and I got what I wanted. It took less than 24 hours and the sellers accepted my offer. Would I regret my impatience years later? Time would tell, but for now that was not important. Mother and I would be living in Carlsbad Springs within a month or two.

The house was going to be mine by mid-October. It was now early September. There remained a lot to do. I wanted to take as many of Mother's belongings as possible. Some pieces of furniture would have to stay in Mother's large farmhouse due to their size. I would move as many things as I could to make her feel more at home.

Now that Mother had decided to move in with me, the house and whatever furniture was left behind would go to Antoine. He had bought the house and farm from her some years earlier. Mother had sole use of the house for free until she either left or passed away.

I organized the move. Denise, who had been with Mother for several years, was also happy, as she had wanted to go back to her own home but did not want to leave Mother alone. Everything worked out for everyone. With guidance from Mother (and from me in the background), Denise packed Mother's things, frequently reminding her that her new home would be smaller than her own house, so that not everything could go. We helped her to focus on determining the furniture she used most often. I suggested to Denise that she observe and make notes about where Mother spent most of her time, which would help determine the furniture that should (and could) be moved.

My sister Andrée went down on the last few days before I arrived with nephews, brothers, and friends to load up furniture. She helped to finish the packing. Having seen the new house, she could explain some of its space constraints.

In late October, a mere six months after starting down this path, I sat at the wheel of a large moving truck, driving to Cowansville. Andrée had driven Mother to her house near Ottawa the previous afternoon. Mother would stay there until everything was moved and organized. That night, I stayed at my brother's place.

The next morning, David arrived with his two sons. Both of my brothers, a few of my friends as well as a neighbour were also there to give us a hand loading the truck. I could not take everything, so choices had to be made. However, we made sure that whatever had been identified by Mother as required was loaded onto the truck.

I wanted to make Mother's stay with me as comfortable as possible. I wanted her to recognize familiar surroundings, even with her limited vision. Mother had beautiful furniture that she got when she married. She also had some that came from her parents or from other relatives. She had a sofa and two chairs that were probably a hundred years old for which she had made some beautiful slipcovers, end tables with leather tops, wonderful marble art deco pieces, and her parents' 19th century oak dining table, a rare piece. We loaded up what I knew would fit in the new house. By early afternoon, I was on my way. My nephew Peter had offered to share the driving back to Ottawa. I was grateful for the company and it gave us an opportunity to talk.

By eight o'clock that night David, his two sons, my friend Richard, and I had unloaded everything. Everyone went home except for Richard. We spent the better part of the night setting up furniture, hanging pictures, and making the place look like home. Some boxes remained in the basement, but I would get to them over the next few weeks. David had spent several days the week before changing the locks, helping me clean, and putting up new curtains. The house had certainly been left in great shape, but there were a few minor changes I wanted to make before Mother arrived.

By early afternoon on Sunday, most of the house was organized and looked lived-in. Richard and I went to the grocery store where he insisted on buying all of the items for the kitchen, from apples to spices, including cooking oil and pasta.

Richard's generosity, to this day, is endless. He and Mother were good friends. He loved her like his own mother and she enjoyed his laughter and good disposition. She treated him like one of her own sons. He would remain a good friend throughout. On several occasions, when I had to be away on a weekend, he drove from Montreal to spend time with her and make sure she had all she needed. Years later he would care for his own aging mother and aunt.

Monday morning, David came in to help me decorate Mother's bedroom—installing the carpet, putting up the curtains, and setting it up to look identical to her room on the farm.

Andrée and David planned to take Mother over on Tuesday at dinnertime. Everything was ready. The decision had been made, arrangements had been made, and the move was complete. Carlsbad Springs was going to be our new home for the foreseeable future. Both our lives were going to change; only time would tell to what degree.

"Today I close the door to the past, open the door to the future, take a deep breath, step on through and start a new chapter in my life." – Anonymous

Chapter 5
The First Dinner

November 2, a day like no other. Yes, I was going to work as I had been doing for several weeks, but this day would be very different. Andrée and David would be bringing Mother to her new home that evening for dinner.

As I walked around the house, making sure everything was perfect, many questions came to mind: Would Mother be happy here? I had made every attempt at making the house comfortable for her; however, she had lived in the same house for 50 years, a house that held so many memories for her. Would she be able to get accustomed to this new yet smaller place? Would I be able to care for her? Would I get used to having an elderly person living with me? Had I made the right decision? How would Mother feel about living with her son? She surely had her own anxieties and anticipations.

What were they? Many questions would be answered over the coming weeks and months.

I left for work knowing I would be back soon as this day would go very quickly. I would be back by five because Andrée would be arriving around six. She had offered to bring a stew, so I would not have to worry about making dinner, a gesture I appreciated.

As soon as I arrived from work, I lit a fire in the fireplace and turned the lights on as it was already starting to get dark outside. Moments later, there was a ring at the door. It was Mother with Andrée and David. I helped Mother in and we all walked into the foyer leading to the living room. She stopped and looked around slowly as I took her coat. She was moving her head around to see where she was and getting her eyes accustomed to the indoor lighting. It took a few minutes for her to get a complete picture of her surroundings.

"Andrée," she said, inquiring about her whereabouts, "why have you brought me back to Cowansville?"

We were all stunned. "But Mother, you are not in Cowansville. This is Jean-François' house and you are in Ottawa."

"But it looks like my old house," she said.

"Yes, Mother," I replied, "it does look a bit like your house. I brought many of your things, so you would be more comfortable. Come, let's walk and I will show you more of the house."

"Oh! A fireplace! Now I know this isn't my old house. I always wanted a fireplace, but François never got around to building one."

As we walked through the living room into the dining room, she recognized the corner hutch that my brother Daniel had made for her to display some of her favourite knick-knacks.

As we got closer to the end of the dining room, she saw what she thought was a large window. I explained that it was a patio door, which led to a large deck. It was too dark now, but we would look at it tomorrow. We then walked into the kitchen. It was somewhat smaller than the one she had, but it was functional—ample counter space and a state-of-the-art stove I had bought especially for her.

An Electric Range/Stove with an Indicator Light

One of the things I had discovered while doing my research in preparation for Mother's arrival was the availability on the market of an electric stove that had an indicator light at the front border of the heating elements. Once that one or more of the heating elements were at a certain degree, it would show a red light, something she would be able to see, thus preventing any unfortunate incidents.

There was also her own refrigerator that had the freezer at the bottom—making it easier for her to access what she needed without having to bend over— a small table for two, and a window behind the sink overlooking the backyard. I can still see her looking outside the kitchen window over the sink back in Cowansville, to predict the weather. If memory serves me right, she was often right on the money.

We continued our walkabout. We took the corridor that led to her bedroom, stopping to look at the bathroom. She noticed that I had decorated it with the same beautiful rose-covered shower curtain she had back at home. Little did she know that the best was yet to come. We entered one of the bedrooms that I had decorated and arranged as a small TV room, with her favourite sitting chair and hassock. She could hardly see what was on the TV, yet she still enjoyed listening to it. We then continued our walk into the "pièce de résistance", her bedroom. I knew this would be her favourite.

I opened the door to her bedroom. I had turned on all the lights. She stopped to look slowly around the room. The room, though a smaller version, was identical to her room back in Cowansville. She could hardly believe it. She focused on me and, with tears in her eyes, moved closer to take me in her arms. With tears of happiness she said, "This is my new home; thank you for having me." We finished the tour of the upstairs and then sat down in the dining room to have dinner. Andrée had already put the stew in the oven to keep it warm.

Quick and Easy Vegetarian Stew
Makes two or three servings

People who love to cook have their favourite stew recipe. The following recipe is mine. If you prefer various kinds of meat, then this might not be for you. However, if you are interested in a stew that is quick and easy to prepare, contains lots of protein, has your favourite vegetables, all at an affordable price, then this recipe is for you. Note: If you prefer, you can use fresh or frozen chicken breasts that you would cook in a skillet prior to adding them to the stew.

Ingredients

1	tsp. olive oil
½	tsp. turmeric
½	tsp. black pepper
½	cup low-salt vegetable broth
2	carrots, sliced
2	parsnips, sliced
2	small turnips, diced
1	medium onion, quartered
6	small potatoes cut in two or 2 medium potatoes cut in 6
4	mushrooms, quartered (optional)
1	package of frozen Gardein[1] meatless beef tips1 to mix with one of the following: Dijon mustard, Pesto, BBQ sauce, or other condiment of your choice plus your favourite fresh or dried herbs (e.g., rosemary, oregano, thyme, etc.)

Preparation

1. *Preheat the oven to 350° F. Coat a small roasting pan with olive oil. Sprinkle the turmeric and the pepper in the pan.*

2. *Wash the vegetables and cut accordingly. Then mix and spread all the vegetables in the roasting pan. Sprinkle your favourite herbs to your taste.*

3. *Pour the ½ cup of vegetable broth over the vegetables. Cover and place in the centre of a preheated oven.*

---

[1]   At the time of publishing, Gardein™ products are usually available in the vegetarian frozen products section.

4. *Cook for 30-40 minutes.*

5. *Carefully remove roasting pan from oven.*

6. *Mix the meatless beef tips with the partially cooked vegetables, cover, and put back in oven for another 20-25 minutes.*

7. *Carefully remove from oven and serve.*

Note: I always cook more vegetables than I actually need and use the rest in a soup. A day or two later, prepare as directed a packet of Knorr™ minestrone soup. When it is almost ready to serve, add the leftover vegetables, a small can of beans (black, kidney, chick, soya, or black-eye), and simmer for 10-12 minutes. With a piece of whole-wheat or multi-grain bread, this will make a great healthy lunch!

Throughout the entire dinner, Mother kept talking about the house and the different things she had seen. She exclaimed over how wonderful it was and how happy she was to be here. Many of my earlier questions seemed to be getting answers. Would everything be okay or was this simply the newness of it all?

Around eight o'clock or so, Andrée and David left to go home. They had a good hour's drive ahead of them and it was getting late. I thanked Andrée for the great meal as we said our goodbyes and acknowledged that we would call each other.

Mother and I continued talking about all sorts of things. She was definitely excited. I let her know that I would be home for a few days to help her familiarize herself with her new surroundings. By about ten o'clock she started to slow down her conversation, so I suggested she go to bed. This was turning out to be a very long day for Mother, as she usually was in bed by eight thirty or nine o'clock. I left the light on in the bathroom, so she could find her way should she need to get up in the night.

After Mom had gone to bed, I decided to sleep in the spare bedroom next to hers to be nearby in case she found herself disoriented during the night. She did get up in the middle of the night, but she turned on the light on her night table, made her way to the bathroom and went back to bed. Nothing unusual occurred during the rest of the night. The next morning, I woke up early, quickly made the bed and went downstairs to take a shower and get dressed. I went up to the kitchen shortly after to get breakfast ready. Around eight o'clock I heard Mother getting up. She went to the bathroom and then slowly made her way into the living room. I watched her and determined that she was a bit disoriented. I walked into the living room from the other side and said good morning. She looked up at me, then smiled, saying, "Bonjour, je suis un peu perdue." I guided her to the kitchen.

I asked her how she had slept and how she felt waking up in this house. She did say that she was a bit lost but that should resolve itself within the next few days, as she got more familiar with the house. We had breakfast together. She preferred toast and coffee. Mother did not have a big appetite, but she ate three meals a day.

Mother and I spent the morning looking at the whole house, and then going outside on the patio. Being November, it was a bit chilly, but she wanted to walk around the house to see the grounds. We had a light lunch and continued talking about various things. I was on the phone for a while with Andrée, who was inquiring about Mother's first night. When I went back into the living room, she had fallen asleep. I let her rest while I did some cleaning up. She woke up about an hour and a half later. She joined me in the kitchen and I showed her where things were, so she could make her own breakfasts and lunches.

During previous years, with the help of Denise, Mom had regained a lot of her independence. She was capable of doing many things for herself. She took care of all her personal needs, got around with the help of a cane, made her own breakfast and, most importantly, took her medication. Denise took care of the major household duties along with lunch and dinner. However, Mother was able to prepare simple meals. My goal was to prepare lunches for her and show her how to reheat them in the microwave. I would be around for dinners.

We looked at various utilitarian appliances that were organized to facilitate her life, so she could maintain her independence as much as possible. The following small appliances and organizational tips where very beneficial to mother's continued independence.

Toaster Oven

The toaster oven was attached to the underside of the cupboard in order to save counter space. The model was equipped with a very large knob on the door that opened downward with the tray automatically sliding outward. Mother had only to open the door, put a couple of slices of bread on the tray, close it and press down on the large lever. Once the toast was ready it would stop, a bell would ring, and Mother could easily open the door and take the toast out without burning herself.

Auto Shut-off One-cup Coffee Maker

The second appliance was a small single-cup coffee machine that I had purchased some time ago for myself at work. Once the water had boiled and filtered through the coffee grinds, the machine would shut off automatically. It was easy to prepare and easy to use. There are even simpler single-serve machines on the market today.

Placement of Items in Cupboards and Refrigerator

The main condiments and items she frequently used were placed within easy reach at eye-level shelves in the cupboard and at the front of the refrigerator. Milk was in a 500 ml (17 oz.) container for easy handling. The arthritis in her hands made handling anything bigger too difficult. She used margarine, so it was in a bright container and it was the creamy smooth style. She loved different fruit preserves, so I provided small jars of it and left the lids only slightly tightened.

For lunch, I made a meat loaf with vegetables and potatoes. Most meals I cooked were four or five portions. Two were eaten during the meal while the other portions were saved for future lunches and possibly dinners if I could not come home in time to cook. Some were in the freezer while there were always two or three choices in the refrigerator section.

I had purchased several one-portion-size dishes with covers in which I put each leftover portion. For each there was a label indicating the content written in big black letters, easier for her to read. On any given day, Mother could choose what she wanted to eat for lunch and put it in the microwave. Mother was not very familiar with this modern appliance, so I explained the basics for safe use.

Using the Microwave Oven

At that time, manufacturers made small dial-style microwave. With this model, I created a temporary stop on the dial mechanism so that when the device was in place, the maximum amount of time available was two minutes[2]. However, when I needed to use the microwave for a longer period, I could remove the device and use as much time as I needed. I had first tried to adapt a more complex push-button model, but it had not been successful. In this case, a much simpler model worked best.

Around six o'clock we had dinner. While I did the dishes, Mother went to change into her nightgown and housecoat. We sat in the TV room listening to a few programs and talking about her first day and how she felt at home. Though she indicated that she was comfortable spending the next day by herself, I had decided to stay and have her go through the different steps for her meals as well as all other activities in the house she wished to engage in. By eight thirty Mother was falling asleep. She went to bed. It had been a very long and exhausting day

---

2 Determining the right time to microwave had been a case of trial and error until I concluded that, based on the containers I had purchased, two minutes was sufficient time to have the food hot but not to the point of burning her tongue.

for her. I retired to my quarters in the basement, also tired. Tomorrow would be a different kind of day, as I would oversee how she managed the various appliances and the house.

Thursday came and went. Mother got up at her usual time, made herself a cup of coffee and a couple of toasts. We chatted for a while, and then she went to get dressed. When it came time to have lunch, she retrieved a dish from the refrigerator, read the label, put it in the microwave and turned the dial. Two minutes later she had a meal in front of her. She even boiled some water to make some tea.

Cordless Kettle

To minimize the chance of an accident, the model purchased sat on its base to boil water; however, once removed from the base, there were no electric wires dangling that might catch somewhere and cause a mishap.

In the afternoon, Mother had a nap while I took care of some of the unopened boxes in the basement. Later that afternoon we went out on the deck for a little while. I described to her my vision for the backyard with the flowerbeds and the vegetable garden. She thought it was a good idea as she also enjoyed fresh vegetables from the garden. We also went downstairs, as she had not yet seen my quarters. It took a few minutes, as there were two sets of steps with a landing in between. She noticed the wood stove and remarked that should there be a power outage, we could still be comfortable.

Large Button Phone

Should she need to contact me, she could use the special large-number-button phone installed in the kitchen. My work number as well as the phone numbers for my sisters and brothers were pre-programmed and stored with names written in large letters. She had tried it out successfully. I felt good about these first few days. Mom was here to stay and everything would be fine.

The whole day went very well as Mother managed the entire household as if she had lived there for months. Tomorrow would be another day and I would call her a few times from work.

Chapter 6
Settling In

The following weeks were dedicated to getting all the support systems in place—providing Mother with everything she needed to ensure her comfort. The first issue at hand was to find a doctor that understood and spoke French who would take Mother on as a patient. Within a few days, through friends and contacts, I was able to find a young doctor who specialized in geriatric care. An appointment was made for the following week. I had been lucky as there had been a cancellation just prior to my call.

The evening before the appointment, I assembled the ingredients for a shepherd's pie and put the pie in the refrigerator. The next morning, I put it in the oven on the timer so that it would heat up for about an hour and be ready when I came home from work.

I was able to leave a few minutes early, so I was home by noon. I prepared a small salad, using various greens, radishes, tomatoes, cucumbers, and celery. For the dressing, I made Mother's famous (at least to our family) salad dressing—a mixture of olive oil, malt vinegar, curry powder, and a sprinkle of stevia or sugar. The recipe for this delightful dressing is unwritten as it all depends on one's taste for each ingredient. I tend to be partial to curry, so I use a little more. If these ingredients sound interesting to you, then give them a try. The proportion of oil to vinegar is standard.

Vegetarian Shepherd's Pie with a twist
Makes 4-6 servings

Shepherd's pie is often seen as a French-Canadian comfort dish, though the name "Pâté chinois" has always seemed to me an unusual name. The traditional dish that I grew up with was made with cooked ground beef with a layer of creamed corn and topped with mashed potatoes and paprika. Though I have made this recipe many times using ground beef, over the years I have been using a meatless product. I find this version more in line with my dietary choices as it is very high in protein, has a reasonable amount of sodium and no fat. The following recipe is made with veggie ground round[3].

---

3 Veggie Ground Round is the name used for the product made by *Yves Veggie Cuisine*™, beefless ground by *Gardein*™. *PC Blue Menu*™ also has a similar quality product.

Ingredients

1	tbsp. oil
1	small onion, diced
4-5	mushrooms, sliced (optional)
1	tbsp. Mrs. Dash™ no-salt table blend seasoning[4]
1	12 oz. (340 g) package meatless ground round
1	can of creamed corn (or mixed vegetables)
1	package scalloped potatoes[5]

Preparation

1. Prepare the scalloped potatoes in the oven as directed however, removing from the oven earlier, around 20-25 minutes.

2. While scalloped potatoes are cooking, heat olive oil in a skillet and cook onions and mushrooms until soft.

3. Add the entire package of meatless ground round and spread evenly with the onions and mushrooms and heat. Add seasoning, mix and heat for 8-9 minutes.

4. After 25 minutes or so, remove the scalloped potatoes from the oven and lower temperature to 350° F.

5. Using an oven-safe deep dish (approx. 6" x 10"), put the mixture of onions, mushrooms, and meatless ground round in the bottom, spread the corn or mixed vegetables evenly over the mixture, then add the nearly fully cooked scalloped potatoes on top.

6. Put in the oven for 15-20 minutes.

7. Serve with a salad.

---

4 For a spicy flavour, use the Mrs. Dash salt-free Southwest Chipotle seasoning.
5 The Knorr™ Side Kick or similar products are often on sale.

Given that the appointment was at two o'clock, we had lots of time to eat and chat before heading out to the doctor's office. After lunch, Mother went to get ready while I put the leftovers away and did the dishes. Mother always cleaned up the kitchen soon after every meal. She hated leaving the counters dirty, so everything was spick-and-span by the time we left.

The drive was only a few minutes and there was ample parking space, given that the clinic was in a small strip mall. After registering at the reception, we sat for a few minutes before Mother's name was called. I helped her to the examination room. The doctor arrived shortly. He was very pleasant and gentle with Mother. He began with a long conversation with Mother and me to get a handle on her medical history, until her medical files could be sent from her previous doctor in Cowansville. He was visibly concerned about the sores on her legs.

He asked me to wait outside while he conducted a complete physical. After a half hour or so, he came out to chat with me while Mother finished getting dressed with the help of the nurse. He explained that he had done a quick analysis of her blood with a glucometer and her blood sugar was very high. He asked me what she had had for lunch before coming to the clinic. He also inquired if I was aware that she had diabetes or if her previous doctor had ever diagnosed this condition. I told him that it had never been communicated or even mentioned.

He proceeded to explain to me that the sores on her legs were probably linked to the diabetes. More tests would need to be done to confirm his suspicion. Not wanting to wait for the test results, he gave me a prescription, which he indicated should be filled as soon as possible, and that Mother should start taking the medication three times a day starting at today's evening meal. He also gave me some suggestions about her diet, proposing to make an appointment for me with a dietician to learn more about diabetes and most importantly the do's and don'ts of shopping and cooking for her condition. Information that would also be very useful for my own dietary needs.

He would contact me as soon as the more in-depth test results came back from the laboratory. In the meantime, I should keep a close watch on what Mother ate. Sweets like chocolate, cookies, and desserts were definitely out.

When Mother came out of the examination room, the doctor spent a few minutes explaining to her what he had told me. She was totally shocked and surprised that her previous doctor had never diagnosed this condition, especially when she realized that the condition of her legs was linked.

The doctor also confirmed what I had been made aware of during my initial research for elder care in the Ottawa area prior to Mother's arrival. Because of her age and her condition, she was eligible to have a nurse come in to change the bandages on her legs. We agreed that three times a week would be great to start off. He would make the necessary arrangements to begin the visits within the next week or so. In a couple of months, he wanted to see Mother again to see how everything was going and see if a different frequency would be appropriate.

The doctor also shared a very important piece of information. Some years before, the province had put in place a program to support elderly people in order that they might stay longer in their homes rather than going to care facilities. The home care program provided a trained professional who would come for up to 3 hours a day from Monday to Friday, up to a maximum of 15 hours a week, to help with any personal needs.

Within a couple of weeks, most of the support resources were in place. The lab tests had confirmed that Mother did indeed have diabetes. I had received a call from the nursing agency to arrange for a first visit to get acquainted and discuss the service that would be provided. A nurse from the Victorian Order of Nurses came by every other day starting Mondays. She would chat with Mother, ask about her health, check her blood pressure, take her pulse, and inquire about any ailment that might cause concern. She then would gently remove the bandages, wash the sores with a saline solution, and put fresh bandages on her legs.

I also made arrangements with the local home care agency to have someone visit twice a week at first, in between the visits by the nurse. The doctor had provided me with the necessary documentation to activate the process. She would arrive mid-morning, help Mother with her personal needs such as bathing and foot care as well as change the bandages on her legs. They would talk about different things throughout. She would sometimes prepare Mother's lunch, though most of the time Mother did that herself. The caregiver would usually leave after lunch.

At first, the caregivers that came varied from time to time, until several months later when I would luck out in getting a gem. As the need to increase the number of hours grew, the agency sent Donna, a wonderful, considerate, and helpful lady who happened to live nearby. She would take care of Mother for many years to come.

Mother did not resist the attention as she had done in the early years of her illness. I remember when she returned to her home in Cowansville after spending many weeks at the Neurological Institute. Mother had been somewhat resistant and she was at times harsh with her companion, to the point where it had taken several weeks and several people before a good relationship finally developed between Mother and a caregiver.

Years later, I would understand and appreciate the importance of good chemistry between the caregiver and the care receiver. Becoming dependent on another person is a difficult situation. Mother had been the caregiver all her life and now she was the one who needed help. Not easy to accept. Her many years with Denise had made this transition much easier.

I knew that Mother would be comfortable in her new home; however, having someone at the house every day reassured me. Mother enjoyed and looked forward to having someone to chat with every day.

In my initial research I had received priceless information from a variety of sources. Several friends and professionals had shared their knowledge and experiences. I had made sure that the furniture was placed in such a way as to give Mother ample room to walk around without obstacles. Mother often took naps in the afternoon. With the days getting dark much earlier and to ensure her safety, timers were installed.

Timers for Lights

As a safety measure, especially for the late autumn, winter, and early spring months, when it gets dark earlier, I installed several timers that have the capacity to have the lights go on and off at specific times. This ensured that Mother could walk about safely.

The home care agency had sent one of their specialists to look at the way I had set up the various rooms that Mother used in order to see if anything could be a hazard to her. She had been quite pleasantly surprised at the way the house was set up; however, she gave me some excellent ideas concerning the bathroom.

Adapting a Bathroom

The changes or adaptations[6] included a non-slip floor, a raised toilet seat, a seat and some non-slip strips in the bathtub, a hand-held showerhead, grab bars on three sides of the bath with another one on the entry side.

On weekends I oversaw the different activities of Mother's routine. When she took a bath, I would stay nearby just in case. I did not want a repeat of the past.

Several years earlier, when Mother was in her house in Cowansville, she normally took a bath when Denise was there to supervise and assist. However, one particular day that she was alone for the day, Mother had decided to take a bath by herself. The bathroom was not equipped with any assistive devices like grab bars or a seat. Once her bath finished, she was unable to get

---

6   Most of these items can be found at hardware stores or at more specialized stores in your area or on the Internet. Search under "Assistive Devices" or "Medical Services."

out of the tub. As she later told us, she tried for several hours to get out but with no success. She let the water out and covered herself with towels. Luckily, Antoine who lived nearby dropped in to say hello and found her in the tub very weak and cold. He helped her out and got her dressed. She was all right after a few hours of warmth. That very day we made changes to her bathroom and insisted that she no longer attempt to do this on her own without supervision. She agreed as she had been very much frightened by the experience.

Other Supports

Other services were also identified to meet Mother's needs. A security medallion that could be activated by pressing on it was linked to a security service in case she fell when there was no one at the house. If the device was activated, the service would call; if there was no answer they would call the first responders or, if none could be reached, the local police.

Donna had provided Mother with the name of a hairdresser who operated a small home-based salon nearby. Whenever Mother wanted a cut or a perm, we would drive over and Mother would have her hair done. The young woman who ran the salon was great and she made Mother laugh. I also discovered some time later that some hairdressers did make house calls.

When Mother wanted to do some shopping, we were but a few minutes from a large shopping mall that had a Sears among a number of other stores. Since Mother walked slowly, I would plan our shopping trips to include a visit to the ladies' room. This prevented any potential incident that might make Mother uncomfortable.

Within a month or so, we had a routine and everything went very well. As Christmas approached, I put up a lot of decorations, including on several trees in the backyard for us to admire all light up in blue and green, a big tree in the house, and garlands around the fireplace as well as several poinsettias at strategic locations in the living room. The two of us spent a quiet yet enjoyable Christmas Day. At her request, I prepared some Cornish hens with apricot-pecan stuffing and all the trimmings. I had found various Christmas recipes for diabetics, or modified some of my own recipes. As long as I minimized the quantity of sugar and carbohydrates, Mother's sugar level stabilized and the sores on her legs began to slowly heal.

I organized a family get-together for New Year's. I cooked up a storm as I usually did and all my sisters and brothers came with their spouses and children. We had a great time. Mother looked wonderful. The day before, she had gone to the hairdresser. She wore a beautiful emerald green gown with gold thread trimming that I had bought for her while on vacation some years before in Morocco. She sat in the blue velvet Queen Anne chair facing the fireplace that was going full blast as everyone arrived. She chatted with everyone, while exchanging hugs and kisses. They all commented on how well she looked.

We ate at about one thirty. I had made all the favourite dishes that I knew my family enjoyed: roast turkey, ham baked in maple syrup, a combination of mashed carrots, parsnips, and onions, broccoli, mashed potatoes, and cranberry sauce.

We also had a galantine[7] that my sister Andrée had prepared. For dessert, we had maple syrup pudding, low-sugar carrot cake, low-sugar banana bread, and a fruit trifle, which was always a favourite with the kids.

After a wonderful afternoon, everyone left to go home since most had several hours of driving before reaching their destination. After everyone had gone, Mother dozed off in her chair while I finished cleaning up. It had been a great day and a new year was starting.

Banana Bread

This banana loaf is probably the easiest recipe you will ever make. The original recipe is with sugar; however, I modified it, using a sweetener[8] instead. Bananas are already very sweet therefore adding sugar makes it too much.

Ingredients

3/4	cup unbleached flour
1/2	cup whole-wheat or multi-grain flour
1	tbsp. ground flax seeds (optional)
1	tsp. baking soda
2	eggs
¼	cup oil
⅓	cup sweetener
2	large ripe bananas (or 3 small ones)

7   A galantine is a mixture of various cooked meats, spices, and gelatine, all placed in a mould that is lined with slices of hard-boiled eggs and sliced pimento-stuffed olives. The colours make the whole dish look quite festive once it is removed from the mould.

8   I have used various sweeteners over the years; however, I now use a more natural product called stevia. I have found that ½ to ¾ the quantity suggested is sufficiently sweet.

¼   cup coarsely chopped walnuts (optional)
¼   cup semi-sweet chocolate chips (optional)

Preparation

1. Preheat oven to 350° F.

2. In a large bowl, sift together the flour and the baking soda and set aside.

3. In a medium bowl, mash bananas and mix in remaining ingredients.

4. Add to dry ingredients, stirring until well blended.

5. Pour into greased loaf pan and bake in preheated oven for approximately 60 minutes or until an inserted toothpick comes out clean.

Chapter 7
Talking About It

The New Year brought a typical winter with lots of snow, wind, and very cold temperatures. The house was very comfortable and Mother thoroughly enjoyed the warmth. She often commented on how cold she had been at the farmhouse during previous winters, having to remain in the kitchen most of the day where it was warmest.

As the weeks passed my comfort level increased as I settled into my new job, various departments were starting to inquire about what I could do to support their needs, which meant that I would be travelling across the country. By the end of January, I felt confident that Mother was totally comfortable with her new surroundings, which coincided nicely with my work schedule of being on the road a couple of days a week. We had talked briefly about my being away once in a while, but I did not talk much more about it.

I always made sure that there were plenty of prepared dishes in the refrigerator and the freezer, that there was either a nurse or a home care provider present for several hours every day. I would call Mother every night after dinner to catch up on the events of her day and mine. I knew she was comfortable because the heating system was programmed to ensure that the house was always around 25 °C (about 80 °F).

My schedule changed from week to week. Some weeks I was around every day while at other times I could be away almost all week. I was, however, home every weekend. It was some time in the spring that Mother broke down. We were having breakfast one Saturday morning and I was talking about my work and how I would be away for several days the following week. She started crying. I was surprised at first and asked what was wrong. She said that nothing was wrong.

"Are you in pain?" I asked.

"No, no. It's that you are never around anymore. You are always away and I'm lonely."

At that very moment I realized that I had not really prepared her for the times I would be away for work. Yes, I had talked briefly about the fact that this new job would involve travelling; however, for the first couple of months I had not travelled at all. She had gotten used to my being around every day for dinner, spending evenings and weekends together. In hindsight, I should have talked more about my trips with Mother.

During my initial research into the role and responsibility of a caregiver, I had been told that a regular routine needed to be set up, that talking about upcoming change that may impact what had become familiar and reliable was important, especially when the change meant that I would not be at home every day. Minor issues may not require this kind of approach; however, my being away for several days at a time was a major change for Mother.

So, we began talking about what was troubling her. She explained how she had concluded that I would not be travelling that much, based on the first few months and that I would be with her more often. Having lived several years with Denise, her live-in companion, she had become accustomed to having someone with whom she could converse throughout the day.

Over the last few months, I had been away two or more days almost every week and she missed having me around. She appreciated having someone come in every day, but it was the evenings that she found to be long and would get lonely. Mother had unfortunately concluded that my absence meant that I was changing my mind about having her live with me.

In turn, I talked about my job and how at first, because I was new, I had to get more familiar with and understand the organization, and by the same token it had to get to know me. I had to prove myself as a valuable contributing member of the organization as my skills could only be used once the people within the organization trusted me. I had crossed that point and now my skills were being requested in different parts of the country. With an organization of over forty thousand people, there were lots of things happening that required my skills.

Over the previous summer months, while Mother was still on the farm, we had often spoken about each other's apprehensions related to her coming to live with me. Travelling for work had been discussed but unfortunately only briefly. For me, this was an issue that was settled and I had seen no need to talk about it when my work schedule changed. Little did I realize the impact it was having on Mother. Unknowingly, I was fuelling her greatest fears—having to go live in a nursing home.

It was an emotional weekend to say the least; however, we both concluded that this was part of my job and that it was part of our reality. I agreed, at her request, to talk more openly about my job and to let her know my travel schedule as much in advance as possible, so she could prepare herself for my absence. Talking things through would be my approach from now on.

Over the coming months, I continued to travel, but I would try to reduce my days away from home. Whenever possible, I would make day trips, leaving early by car or air and coming back before Mother had gone to bed. Mother's reaction to my absence bothered me a lot. Though I knew that this was part of my work and that after our conversation about the issue she seemed to be fine with it, I still worried about it. I did not want Mother to think that I did not love her, nor did I want her to think that I was going to put her in a nursing home.

Whenever I did my shopping or errands, Mother would accompany me when she felt up to it; however, I decided that I would limit my social activities to a strict minimum. That went on for several months.

The problem with my decision was that I now was, in my mind, blaming Mother for my limited social life. I would get invited to dinner, movies, or simply going for coffee with some of my friends, but I declined, saying that I had other commitments.

Though the first winter in Carlsbad Springs had been a cold one, we had been very comfortable in our new home. Downstairs, whenever I was in the house, I had a fire going in the stove while upstairs I kept the temperature at a level where Mother did not have to wear a sweater.

A couple of times a week, I would walk through the heavy snow in the backyard to fill the birdfeeders that I had installed in late autumn. There was one for the smaller birds like chickadees, goldfinches, purple finches, and juncos, and two larger feeders for the boisterous blue jays, woodpeckers, and the occasional shy cardinal, not forgetting the cooing mourning doves that always came in pairs at first light.

My years in the country with Bea had given me an appreciation for the different species of birds that spent the cold winters with us. Of course the squirrels always tried to outsmart the devices that were meant to prevent them from accessing the feed. Through perseverance they always managed to make it to the top of the feeders to eat the precious sunflower seeds.

Winter and spring had come and gone. By mid-April, there was almost no snow and the grass was beginning to take on different shades of green among the brown spots left by the cold and the snow. Over the coming weeks I would start working on one or two of my projects for the backyard while at the same time trying to figure out what to do about the need to be away on business.

"Loneliness does not come from having no people around you, but from being unable to communicate the things that seem important to you." – Carl Jung

Chapter 8
The Ladies' Room Incident

Though our first summer together was very busy with some minor renovations on the house and my work, there was time for a special event. Mother's birthday was at the end of June. As I had done for many years, I started several weeks in advance to organize her birthday party. Though I was not hiding it from Mother, I was keeping the affair a bit low-key. However, one Saturday morning, after I had finished a phone conversation with my brother Daniel, she came into the kitchen and mentioned that she would need to go shopping to get a new summer dress for the birthday party.

Trying to be coy about the whole thing, I said, "De quelle fête parles-tu, maman?"

She looked at me with a look only Mother could give and replied, "My birthday party, of course. I can hear you when you are talking to your brothers and sisters on the phone."

Well, you could have knocked me over with a feather. I now realized that Mother was very aware of everything that went on in the household. It all made sense now. I did not have to worry; she was doing fine in her new home. I started to laugh, telling her that if I wanted to have secrets I would have to be smarter.

She looked at me and said, "You can try, but remember, I know you as if I had knitted you myself."

We laughed. Then she said, "I would like to go shopping for a new outfit. Can we go this afternoon?"

"Of course. We can leave around two o'clock."

"Excellent, je vais allez me préparer."

It had been nearly eight months since Mother had come to live with me. She was getting around the house with much greater ease compared to when she first arrived. For the longest time, she had walked with a specialized cane, the kind with four small legs at the bottom to keep it upright at all times. She had begun walking with a regular cane, but it often fell and she struggled to pick it up, so we had gotten her the four-legged one. The sores on her legs that had been infected and painful were healed. Though she usually still walked with the aid of her cane, I noticed that she often walked without it.

Later, we left for the shopping mall to pick out a new dress for her birthday. Of course, the first stop would be Sears. We drove to the mall and parked near the

Sears side entrance. This is where we would find ladies' apparel as well as being within easy access of the ladies' room. We walked around for a while, looking at different items.

Not finding anything she really liked, Mother asked that I take her to the area where we could look at the catalogues—the regular annual issue and the summer issue. Because of her limited vision, we spent a fair bit of time going through the different issues. I would ask her to describe what she might like—the style, the colour, and so on.

We went through the many pages of the spring/summer issue. When we were both almost ready to abandon our search and go to another store in the mall, I put the catalogue back on the counter and noticed a thin flyer with a picture of two models wearing beautiful outfits, one in azure blue and the other in pink. The ensemble was a three-quarter-length flowing skirt with matching blouse. I showed Mother and she, moving her head in a kind of circular motion, was able to see what had attracted my attention. She said, "C'est exactement ce que je cherchais."

We had found what she was looking for and in colours she liked. We put the order in at the counter. Mother decided to order two sets, one of each colour. The saleswoman informed us that the order should be delivered in a couple of weeks, just in time for Mother's birthday party.

We started to walk back through the store toward the car. As we were nearing the door to go out, Mother mentioned that she had to go the ladies' room. I escorted her as I usually did and waited outside. Several minutes passed and she did not come out and neither did anyone else, so I slowly opened the door and asked, "Est-ce que ça va, maman?"

"Je ne suis pas capable de sortir."

"What do you mean you can't come out? Why not?"

"Well, I locked the door and now I can't unlock it."

I called out to see if there was anyone else in the washroom, but there was no answer. I looked around the area and still saw no one to help me, so I walked in and made my way to the stall occupied by Mother.

I surveyed the lock in the other cubicle and quickly ascertained that it locked by turning clockwise, thus would unlock counter clockwise. Mother's hands were not very strong and therefore she could not manage the rotating movement. The easiest thing for me to do was to get on my back, crawl under the door and unlock the door. A relatively easy task, I thought. Maybe not!

I got in position, asked Mother to step back, and then slid under the door. As I struggled to reach the knob, a woman entered the washroom, saw me, or rather, she saw a pair of men's legs sticking out from under the door. She started to scream and yell and began to kick me, uttering some choice words. I started yelling back that I was trying to get my mother out because she was stuck; however, she did not hear me and continued kicking me and telling me to get out of there.

I called out to Mother to tell her that it was okay, that I was her son and that she was locked in. She did that, but she spoke in French, which the woman did not understand.

"En anglais, Maman, en anglais," I told her.

She repeated the plea in English and the woman stopped abruptly, and said, "What did you say?"

So Mother said it again. I proceeded to unlock the door and slide out. Mother came out, explaining to the woman that she had locked herself in and could not get out.

The woman looked at me and apologized, saying, "What was I to think? I am really sorry."

I reassured her that it certainly was not her fault and under the circumstances it was probably a normal reaction on her part. We said goodbye and silently walked back to the car. A few minutes out of the parking lot, the silence was broken. Mother apologized for the whole thing. I reassured her that it was certainly not her fault. Things like that happen and no harm was done. I was a bit shaken by the entire ordeal; however, I kept my thoughts to myself because I did not want Mother to feel bad as it was not her fault and everything had turned out all right, I guess.

At the time, we agreed that neither of us would speak of the incident to anyone, mostly because of the embarrassment. Besides, I did not look forward to the possible ridicule that might come of this story. After that incident, I replaced all of the rotating doorknobs in the house with lever-type handles, which were much easier to use, thus preventing any future mishaps, in our home at least. At the time, I did not find the incident very funny, but today, as I write these words, I find the whole thing hilarious.

Chapter 9
Feeling Trapped

Throughout the spring and summer months, I worked on my projects. I started in mid-May with a vegetable garden. The house was situated on a green belt, a several-kilometre-wide strip of undeveloped land with trees, bogs, streams, and marshes. The green belt was home to many different species of animals and birds that surround the greater Ottawa area. A handful of houses and farms—built before the land was declared a conservation area—popped up here and there. I had a neighbour on one side of the house and a few across the road, but that was it. The backyard was about an acre in size and it had never really been finished and landscaped.

After choosing an area that received the greatest amount of sun, I removed the sod, and then added some topsoil and a little bit of sheep manure. I had grown up on a farm that had several hundred sheep and goats as well as a variety of other farm animals. Every fall we would spread manure on all the fields that would be ploughed as well as the garden area, in preparation for the next seeding season. Given that this was the first time I was preparing a garden, I made sure that the soil and the manure would be very well mixed together before seeding or planting. Otherwise it would be too strong and would have a burning effect. About a week or so later, during the long weekend in May, I planted small tomato and cucumber plants as well as seeds for beans, peas, radishes, and lettuce, finishing off with some small onions. This would be my first attempt at growing more than herbs and tomatoes since leaving the farm.

As the weeks passed, I watered my little plot of land, and, with the water and the warmth of the sun, the plants started to grow; little sprouts pierced the ground and started taking shape. Radishes and green onions were first, followed by lettuce, beans, and peas. The tomato plants flowered; then small green tomatoes started to take shape and over the weeks that followed we had fresh red juicy tomatoes.

As for the cucumbers... well, this first attempt would not be as fruitful as expected, but I did manage to get a few. I had forgotten a small detail from my years on the farm. Cucumbers like other "gourd" varieties need lots of water. A trick we used on the farm was to make sure that at least one end of the vine-like streamers was cut and gently held down in a small plastic container constantly filled with water, thus ensuring a better crop. All in all, it was a fun experience with tasty results.

Following the conversation with Mother about her reaction to my travelling for work, I had become a kind of hermit—at least, that is what my friends were concluding. Though I did not want to be away more than I had to be, I missed going to the movies or out with friends. In a way, I felt somewhat trapped. Most of the time I rationalized the whole thing and carried on with my life, caring for Mother the best I could and being the best at what I did at work. However, there were times when I got a little depressed and wondered what I had gotten myself into.

I was in my forties with a great career, willingly caring for my aging mother, yet with not much of a social life. What was I to do about it? I certainly could not change my mind and put Mother in a home for seniors. I certainly was not ready to go down that road. I pondered the issue in my mind throughout the summer.

During my summer vacation, I decided to stay around the house and do a few renovations. Two major projects required my immediate attention before the next winter. First, the windows; they were an older model and were certainly not energy efficient, especially those in the basement, the kitchen, and Mother's bedroom as well as the patio door. Second, the shingles on the roof were showing signs of wear and tear and would need to be replaced before a major leak occurred. These projects would keep me busy and give me time to think of how I was going to resolve the issue of my social life—or lack of it.

All the necessary renovations were concluded before the change in seasons and the cold weather. Due to the cost, I replaced only the windows in the basement, Mother's bedroom, and the kitchen; the rest would be completed the following summer. As for my thinking process about my feeling trapped… well, I had arrived at what I thought would be a viable solution.

Given that Mother was usually in bed by nine o'clock, I decided that on weekends I certainly could make it out to a late show or meet up with friends. So, I started to play a game. When I wanted to do something, usually on a Friday or Saturday, I would leave my car in the driveway close to the road. Once Mother had gone to bed and was asleep, I would go downstairs, quietly get ready, sneak out of the house, open the car door on the driver's side, and push the car out onto the street away from the house. Then I would get in, start the car, and go on my way. On a couple of occasions one of the neighbours saw me and I could only imagine what they thought I was doing at that hour.

In October I went to a Halloween party. As usual, I had waited till Mother had fallen asleep—or so I thought— and then I had gone out. The next morning, I had come up for breakfast after Mother had already eaten. I made myself some coffee and something to eat and joined Mother in the living room. We chatted for a few minutes.

Then out of nowhere she said, "Did you have a nice evening last night?"

I froze. "What do you mean?" I responded, trying to be calm about it.

"I heard you leave around eleven, so I figured you were going out. Actually," she said, "now and then I hear you leave late in the evening after I've gone to bed. On occasion I even hear you come home. Tell me Jean-François, I hope you are not sneaking out or something. You're

not a child and if you want to go out then you should!
I may be blind, but I am not deaf. I can still hear what
goes on."

At this point I started to laugh. I could not believe what
I was hearing. All the time I was trying to be so quiet
when I went out, Mother new exactly what was going
on.

I explained that I had actually been sneaking out
because I needed to be with my friends now and then,
but I did not want her to feel abandoned. We both had a
good laugh about it. From then on when I wanted to go
out, I did, or if I wasn't going to come home right after
work I would simply call her up to let her know and that
would be the end of it.

As time went on, both of us learned more and more
about the importance of talking things through before
they became a misunderstanding. Mother looked like
she was happy and certainly expressed it frequently. She
had been independent all her life and she had raised a
family through hard times. Now she needed me, but
not for everything. Whatever I could do that permitted
her to be in control, the happier she was. When I did
do things for her, it had to be done subtly and without
fanfare. She needed to feel independent and in control
and that was fine with me.

Clear
Continual
Consistent
Communication

Chapter 10
Memories of Years Past

Throughout the months, we often had long conversations during dinner and in the evening about living on the farm in Cowansville—the day-to-day challenges, my growing up, my school experiences, and family gatherings. Because the farm was located five kilometres (about three miles) from the village, every trip was planned and organized, especially during the more difficult seasons of the year (late fall to late spring) when the road was not passable by car.

Horse-drawn buggies and sleighs were once common modes of transportation as well as tractors and wagons when they were not used for farming. It was in the mid to late 1950s that the county constructed better roads with regular maintenance. After that, the roads became passable most of the time, regardless of the season. The family car was a station wagon with plenty of room for the whole family.

Mother often talked about events that transpired during my earlier years of growing up, but most often these events were not familiar to me. It seemed that I was missing a part of my childhood. I soon realized that the events she talked about were all during my pre-teen years.

Shortly after my twelfth birthday, I had begun to experience an unusually painful bellyache—much more than one might get from eating too much. The pain was focused more on my right side, so the doctor had been called in. (In those days, doctors actually made house calls.) The roads were not very good at that time of year due to the rain and it had taken a while for the doctor to get from the village to the house. Shortly after his arrival he had determined what was causing the pain. I was rushed to the hospital with acute appendicitis. During my recovery in the hospital, I contracted rheumatic fever[9], which kept me there for longer than anticipated.

Eventually I went back home, but I was laid up for many months. Some days I would not be able to walk, as all the joints in my legs or hips were inflamed. Other days, I could not move my arms or hands. The painful inflammation tended to move around wherever there were joints. On days I could not walk, my brothers would carry me down to the TV room and set me up on the sofa, where I spent most of the day. For nearly a year, my time was spent between home and the doctor's office. Somehow, I had forgotten or blocked off many of my memories of my early years.

---

9 Rheumatic fever is an autoimmune disease that may occur after a streptococcal throat infection, causing inflammatory lesions in connective tissue, especially that of the heart, joints, blood vessels, and subcutaneous tissue. Reference: http://www.medicinenet.com/rheumatic_fever/article.htm

Though Mother had some difficulty remembering daily events, when it came to the past she was able to recall almost everything. One particular incident that she shared with me was the time my two older brothers took on the challenge of teaching me to ride a bike. The farm was situated in an area that was very hilly. In fact, that area has several peaks and valleys that are probably part of the Appalachian Mountains.

My brothers took me on one part of the road that had a downward slope toward the house. At the top of the slope I got on the bike and, as they helped me keep my balance, I pedalled toward the entrance to the yard. However, there was one thing that my brothers had left out of their training and instructions—how to apply the brakes by back-pedalling. As I started to turn into the entrance to the yard, I misjudged the angle and my speed and my bike climbed up the huge elm tree that was situated on the corner.

As the roots extended out from the tree, the wheel of the bike simply followed the gentle slope and I went up a couple of metres (about 6 feet) before falling downward like a sack, much to Mother's horror. Everyone ran toward me to see how I was doing. Yes, I was crying, not because I was hurt but because of my pride.

As time went on, I did master all aspects of bicycle riding and my bike became a useful mode of transportation throughout much of my life. Even now I often go cycling during the spring, summer, and fall months. Like my older siblings, I had to wait till I was twenty-one to get my driver's license, as that was the age one could get it without having a parent's signature.

In those days, teenage children driving tractors on quiet rural roads was not an issue as it is today. However, driving a car on main highways was not possible until a certain age. As I often hear about the increase in accidents by younger drivers, I sometimes think that maybe the driving age should go back to twenty-one.

Listening to Mother talk about all these events—the family gatherings as well as all sorts of things that transpired when I was growing up—was great. Some were sad and some were hilarious; however, all contributed to the creation of a strong bond with my mother. Many of these events had been lost to me during my illness. Other stories that Mother told me were about the many family gatherings, more specifically those during the December holidays. This was a time when our entire family enjoyed good times and good food together at the farm, hosting uncles, aunts, and cousins for nearly two weeks. As a kid and a teenager, I welcomed having other people of the same age around.

Christmas itself was a family-oriented event, with midnight mass on Christmas Eve followed by a typical French Canadian "réveillon". Eventually, we would go to bed, waking up a few hours later to do chores—milking the cows and feeding them as well as the sheep, goats, etc., as they could not wait. We would always discover our Christmas stockings filled with sweets at the foot of our beds.

After chores, we came back to a house filled with the delightful smells of fresh buckwheat pancakes, maple syrup, scrambled eggs, and bacon. With such a large family it was not feasible for Mother to prepare eggs to everyone's specific taste, so scrambled was the alternative as everyone love them cooked in that fashion.

Scrambled Eggs Parmesan
Makes two servings

Scrambled eggs for breakfast are common in most households and restaurants. One trick I discovered a number of years back is to add other ingredients to give the eggs a zestier flavour.

Ingredients

1	tsp. vegetable oil, margarine, or butter
4	eggs or 250 grams of egg mixture
¼	cup milk or cream (optional)
4	tbsp. grated Parmesan cheese
1	tbsp. fresh chopped chives (optional) or
1	tsp. Mrs. Dash™ salt-free original (optional)

Preparation

1. Coat medium frying pan with oil and bring to medium heat.
2. In a bowl, mix eggs with a fork or pour egg mixture.
3. Blend in ¼ cup of milk or cream.
4. Add grated Parmesan cheese and chives or salt-free spices.
5. Pour in frying pan and scramble to your preferred consistency.
6. Serve with toast, bagels, or croissants and preferred condiments.

We enjoyed the day in various ways: cross-country and downhill skiing, snowshoeing, and sliding down a steep hill behind the house on old pieces of cardboard. When we were able to convince Father, we would go skijoring—a fun activity where we would be on skis and holding on to ropes attached to the tractor while Father drove, pulling us from one end of the property to the other. While we played and had fun, Mother and my sisters (when they got older) would be preparing the evening feast with all the trimmings.

In later years, I would actively participate in these preparations. Mother always insisted that all her children, the girls and the boys, learn to clean house, cook, and do minor sewing tasks such as sewing buttons back on shirts or pants. She wanted all of us to be independent and to be able to help around the house.

Within a day or two after Christmas, the house would be bustling with people. Aunts, uncles, and cousins would arrive by train and my father would pick them up at the station with the horse-drawn sleigh. They would stay with us for a week to ten days. It was not unusual for us to host twenty or more relatives at these get-togethers.

With seven bedrooms and more beds than I can remember, some of us would double up while some slept on sofas. It was a wonderful time. Great fun, great food, lots of outdoor activities like the ones I have described as well as building snow forts for snowball fights. After dinner there would be all sorts of games while the adults played cards. Getting the kids to bed was a challenge every night. None of us wanted to go to bed for fear of missing out on the fun.

Then there were all the times spent working on the farm. In my family, we were brought up in such a way that until age seven, we were kids and we behaved as kids. We went to school, had a few chores to do, and played.

However, on our seventh birthday, we became a young man or a young woman. This is when we took on more responsibilities in order to contribute to the family and the farm. The girls helped Mother around the house and, being thirteen and fourteen years older than I, they also helped bring me up. To my two sisters, I was like a doll they played with. I am somewhat glad that I do not remember those details.

In the mid-1950s, Father bought what was considered a state-of-the-art film camera at the time—a Super8. For many years and at different events, Father, Mother or my older siblings would film what we did. Lucky for our family, my brother Daniel transferred all these old style clips on compact disks in order to still view them on occasion. I have clips of my father, my brothers, my sisters, and me travelling from one part of the farm to the other, some driving a tractor, with my mother filming the parade. Other clips show each and every one of us at one point either cutting, raking, or baling hay, or in the wagon behind, catching the bales of hay and placing them securely. There were also clips of us doing the less-desirable chores, such as cleaning the barns and spreading manure in the fields.

Other clips show my brothers coming back from a trip as crew on a ship delivering goods along the eastern and northern coasts, my siblings' weddings, and them visiting the farm with their growing families. Some clips show aunts, uncles, cousins, nephews, and nieces helping out on the farm. Farming was hard work, but we had fun doing it and we learned a lot—many things that greatly helped us into adulthood.

All these memories—some favourable and some not so much, some lost and then rediscovered—are probably the greatest treasures I will ever have from my mother. The time spent reminiscing with her helped me understand many things about my family and me and gave me a more balanced perspective of the world around me.

After all, Mother was a natural born storyteller who enjoyed sharing details. To this day, I believe I have inherited her skills as I find that in my work as a trainer and facilitator, I do have a tendency to tell stories that help my listeners better anchor concepts or ideas.

Chapter 11
Spaghetti Night

Whether I was at home for dinner or away on a business trip, there was always plenty of food in the house. There usually were three or four different meals in the refrigerator and another five or six in the freezer, all clearly labelled for Mother to read and choose what she preferred.

When I would be away on business for several days at a time, I had made an arrangement with Donna that she would cook a meal at lunchtime so as not to reduce the number of prepared meals. I later found out that on most of these occasions, Mother had insisted on doing the cooking herself. Therefore, Donna guided and helped Mother in preparing the meals, ensuring that everything was done safely. Depending on her appetite, Mother would prepare some soup and a sandwich or an omelette with toast.

I did not cook pasta very often, as the carbohydrates were not too good for either one of us. So when I did prepare a pasta dish like macaroni or lasagna, I always made it with lots of vegetables, with or without meat. In those days, there were very few products on the market that were meatless but with lots of protein. The 21st century brought on the market many products made with legumes, soybeans, and various grains that provide alternatives to meat for dishes like tacos, burritos, shepherd's pie, curries, and various pasta sauces.

One night, after a particularly long and demanding day, I came home a bit tired and did not have the energy to prepare a meal as I would normally. My usual approach to food preparation was to cook four portions. It could be roast chicken, beef or pork, meat loaf, a stew, or a stir-fry, which Mother particularly loved. After our meal, I would put the leftover portions in microwave safe dishes, clearly indicating the content and date, then put one in the freezer and the other in the refrigerator.

That night I decided to make spaghetti. It was quick and easy and I had not made any since Mother had moved in with me. I had some tomato and mushroom sauce I had purchased some time before. I had a few mushrooms in the fridge, so I cleaned and sliced them before sautéing them with a bit of garlic. I put the spaghetti in boiling water and heated up the sauce. When dinner was nearly ready, I invited Mother to come and eat. She carried out her normal routine of getting a glass of water and taking her pills.

I placed a reasonable portion of pasta in the middle of the plate, added a couple of ladles of sauce and covered the whole thing with the mushrooms. After putting

Mother's plate in front of her, I cut everything in small pieces to make it easier for her. Mother watched me and said, "Qu'est-ce que c'est?"

I responded, "It's spaghetti with a tomato and mushroom sauce."

To my surprise she said, "What is spaghetti?"

My jaw dropped. "Mother, you know what spaghetti is—it's pasta!"

"No, I don't," she replied. "I've heard about it, but I've never tasted it."

Now, that seemed odd to me. As I went back into my own memories of growing up, I could not actually remember any specific times when we ate spaghetti. Were we both having a mental block? Mother made probably the best macaroni in the world, but maybe that was the extent of the pasta she served.

I explained that spaghetti was like macaroni, but instead of being little elbow-shaped tubes it was long thin strands. Mother was not finicky, so she ate it. She loved it.

"Mais c'est donc bon! It's so good!" she said.

From that day on, spaghetti was on the menu at least a couple of times a month. I would vary the sauces, sometimes using her own meat-and-tomato sauce she used for her famous macaroni. Fond memories race through my mind, every single time I eat spaghetti.

Meatless Pasta Sauce
Makes 5-6 servings

Though I have often tried to reproduce my mother's sauce, it was never exactly like hers. The recipe was in her head and though she tried to guide me through it on a couple of occasions, it was never the same. Out of kindness, she would say, "c'est presque pareil," its almost the same.

A few years back, a good friend who is vegetarian prepared this pasta sauce. I was surprised when he served it at a gathering of friends, as I knew that he did not eat meat. I thought he was making an exception for this event. It was after the meal was over that he announced to all the guests that the sauce was meatless. This is an easy recipe to make and it can be frozen for later consumption.

Ingredients

2	tbsp. vegetable oil
2	medium onions, diced
1	medium pepper, diced or chunks (green, red, yellow, or orange, or a mixture of several)
2	cups diced mushrooms
2	tbsp. minced garlic or to taste
1	28 oz. can diced tomatoes
1	12 oz. (340 g) package meatless ground round
¼	cup fresh coriander (or dried leaves)
2	tbsp. Italian spices (or mix and match your favourite spices)

No salt is required as there is already some in the ground round and in the Italian spices mixture.

Preparation

1. *In a medium or large saucepan, heat the vegetable oil and sauté the onions until soft and translucent.*

2. *Add the peppers and mushrooms and continue sautéing, adding the garlic and spices to the mixture.*

3. *Add the tomatoes and continue stirring for 3-4 minutes.*

4. *Add the meatless ground round and stir until well blended.*

5. *Cover and let simmer at medium-low for 15-20 minutes.*

6. *Prepare your favourite pasta. Depending on your choice of pasta, you can blend the mixture with the pasta (e.g., macaroni) or put pasta on plates and put an appropriate amount of sauce on top.*

7. *(Optional) Sprinkle with Parmesan cheese and/or hot peppers and serve.*

As fall turned into winter, we settled in the comfort of the house. We limited travel to weekly grocery shopping, doctor's appointments, and the occasional shopping trip. In the months that led up to Mother's moving in with me, we had many conversations about numerous topics and situations that we were likely to encounter when we lived together.

One of those was the financial impact on both Mother and me. We had agreed to a monthly amount that she would pay me to cover part of her primary living expenses. One of my sisters, due to situations and events that had transpired a couple of years prior and on the request of mother, had accepted at that time to manage Mother's finances.

Generally, the arrangement worked out. On occasion there would be some challenges, but I managed to cover the extra costs. It was somewhat inconvenient, but it kept the peace. There had been a few times when Mother wanted some money for a particular reason—such as for a new dress or to pay for lunch when we went out shopping—and she had to ask her daughter to get the extra money out of her account. She had on occasion experienced some resistance and even been refused.

Many years before, Mother had gotten dentures. Eating comfortably with them was now somewhat difficult as they were over ten years old and did not fit as well as they did originally. New ones would be an extra expense. A request for the money had been refused. Mother had been very disappointed and upset with the response. In order to keep the relationship viable, I had paid for the new dentures. Though this had been an uncomfortable solution for Mother, she had appreciated the gesture as well as the increased comfort with her new dentures.

Not long after that incident and at her request, I set up a joint bank account for her in a nearby bank. She also asked me to write to the government to have her pension and Old Age Security deposited in that account. This incurred quite a reaction from my sister, who accused me of interfering. I reminded her that, though she was the overseer of Mother's finances, she was not being reasonable in her responses to Mother's personal needs.

The relationship between Mother and daughter—as well as between sister and brother—became strained to say the least. I now realize that while I was doing

Mother's bidding, I should also have informed my sister of Mother's intentions so as to mitigate the impact.

As we got closer to the Christmas season, invitations went out to everyone to come for a New Year's lunch. That year only a few came, giving prior engagements and the distance to travel as reasons for their absence; however, deep down I knew that the events of the previous months had played a part.

As for the joint bank account that I had set up for Mother, a lighter side did come of it, besides her being able to access some of her funds when she wanted. A month or so after her account was activated and her pension cheques were direct-deposited, we went to the branch to get a card in order for Mother to access her account whenever she desired. The teller set up the card with a temporary password and then asked that we go to the automated teller machine (ATM) to change the password to her own choice. After signing the appropriate documents, we made our way to the ATM. Mother asked me to choose a password as I would always be with her anyway and she might forget. She also asked me to get her some money.

As I went through the different steps, I saw Mother looking behind the machine. The money came out and I retrieved her card, so she could put it in her purse. She looked at me and said, "I could not see the teller behind the machine; she is very fast." I looked at her in dismay, then realized that Mother, throughout her entire life, had only interacted directly with a person at the bank and that the ATM was totally foreign to her. What I took for granted was very different for a person of my mother's generation.

As we walked back to the car, I explained the whole process of an ATM. She was speechless, as it did not really make sense at all. It would take several visits over the coming months for the concept to sink in. Technology with all of its advancements was something to be further explained and eventually either understood or tolerated. Luckily, home computers, tablets, and cell phones were still in the future for both of us.

"Technology—the knack of so arranging the world that we don't have to experience it." – Max Frisch

Chapter 12
The Corset Affair

It had now been almost a year and a half since Mother moved in with me. Donna came in every day so that Mother would have some companionship. I had also negotiated with her to stay an extra two hours a day for a total of five to help Mother with her personal care. I had given her a set of keys so that she could come and go easily. She offered to do some house cleaning as she found that she was not fully occupied during these five hours. At first I was a bit uncomfortable with this, but she insisted, saying that she needed to keep busy when Mother was taking a nap. As time went on, not only did she manage to provide Mother with all she needed, she also cleaned the house every week, washed all of our clothes, and on top of all that, did a thorough spring cleaning which included washing all the windows inside.

One day when I came home from work, I found a message that Donna had left me in my room. This was not unusual as she would do so on occasion when there was something that I had either asked for or an event had occurred which she felt I needed to be aware of. However, this note would prove to be different in nature. As Donna was doing the wash that day, Mother had asked her to wash her corset and brassiere and to try and fix them, as they were quite worn. Since having her first child in the 1930s, Mother had been wearing a very wide corset with thin metal boning inserted into channels and eyelets that used laces for tightening around her hips. She also wore a brassiere that was very wide which fitted over the corset. Such garments were no longer available on the market, so she had been repairing them over the years. But, as Donna stated, this was no longer possible. She indicated that she had explained this to Mother. However, she was unsure as to whether Mother was going to discuss it with me to explore other alternatives.

I decided I would wait till the weekend before I said anything, thus giving Mother enough time to think about it and possibly bring up the subject up herself.

Throughout the rest of the week, Mother did not say anything to me about it, so I waited.

On Saturday morning, I got up early to do a bit of cooking, starting with a batch of blueberry bran muffins. While those baked, I prepared some of my parmesan scrambled eggs that Mother liked very much and made a small pot of coffee. I guess the aromas found their way to Mother's bedroom, as she came out just as I was taking the muffins out of the oven. She asked what I was preparing, so I described the piping hot muffins that were on the cooling rack on the kitchen counter along with the scrambled eggs. By her reaction I could see that the morning's fare pleased her. She walked over to the cupboard to get her medication.

Soon after her arrival I had purchased a pill dispenser that was divided into seven strips, clearly marked from Sunday to Saturday, and each day was divided into different times of the day. This made it easier for her to take her medication daily and at the right time.[10]

Blueberry Bran Muffins
Makes 6 medium or 12 small muffins

When I had a small bistro in Montreal, I used to buy pails of pre-made mixtures to prepare muffins. They did not sell very well as they had an artificial taste to them, so I had gone into my recipe books and found something that I had adapted to fit my needs. The recipe that follows has been adapted to reduce the sugar content.

Ingredients

1½	cups All-Bran cereal
1	cup buttermilk[11]
⅓	cup vegetable oil
1	egg
½	cup sweetener
½	tsp. vanilla extract
½	cup all-purpose flour
½	cup whole-wheat flour
1	tsp. baking soda

---

10   Today pharmacies can now prepare a week's or multiple weeks of medication ahead of time. Ask your pharmacist for further details.
11   If none available, you can make your own by putting 1 tablespoon of lemon juice or white vinegar in a measuring cup and filling to a cup with milk. Let stand for 3-4 minutes.

1	tsp. baking powder
¼	tsp. salt
1	cup fresh blueberries (You can also use any fresh berry you have on hand)

Preparation

1. Preheat oven to 375° F. Grease muffin tin or line with paper muffin cups.

2. Blend together the bran and buttermilk and let stand for 10 minutes.

3. Beat together the oil, egg, sweetener, and vanilla and blend in with the buttermilk/bran mixture.

4. Sift together the flour, baking soda, baking powder, and salt and blend in with the buttermilk/bran mixture.

5. Fold in blueberries and spoon batter into the muffin tin.

6. Bake for 15-20 minutes or until a toothpick inserted into the centre comes out clean. Let cool and savour!

We had a good breakfast and a good conversation, talking about different things.

After pausing for a few moments, she brought up the subject. As anticipated, she had put some thought into it and talked—though with some discomfort—about her beyond-repair undergarments. She described the episode that Donna had written to me about and was wondering if we could go to the store to see what alternatives might be available. Having anticipated such a request, I proposed that we get ready and get going as soon as possible. That way we could also do some grocery shopping before the stores got too busy.

As usual, Sears was the store of choice. First we would check what was available on display and see if there was anything different from what was in the catalogue. If that failed, then we would try the other stores in the mall that sold women's apparel. After a quick stop at the bathroom (by then, Mother had agreed that she would not be locking the door to the stall in order to prevent a repeat of the past), we walked over to the women's apparel section.

I sat her down in one of the change rooms while I went to the different rows of undergarments looking for suitable alternatives. Not knowing what size Mother wore, I simply took different sizes of various models. As I was walking back to the change room, a saleswoman intercepted me. She looked me up and down and asked abruptly what I was doing with the boxes.

I said, "My mother is in need of some new undergarments and, because she is blind and somewhat fragile, I am bringing these to her in the change room."

She looked at me and said, "Sure, that's what they all say!"

"What are you implying by that?" I replied.

She proceeded to tell me that either I am in the process of stealing those items or that I want to try them on myself. I was shocked that I was being accused that way.

I looked her right in the eye and said, "Fine. Then come with me and I will be glad to introduce you to my mother."

"I don't have time to waste," she replied.

"Then I want to see the manager."

"No, you should give me those items and leave the store."

"No, madam, I insist."

So she begrudgingly agreed to follow me to the change rooms. There, I knocked on the door saying, "Maman, puis-je entrer?"

"Oui," she replied.

I opened the door and introduced Mother to the saleswoman. Her jaw dropped. She looked at me and apologized profusely for her behaviour. Then she offered to take care of Mother personally. I nodded yes, walked away and sat nearby, still a bit upset at the way I had been treated.

For nearly an hour she went back and forth between the shelves and the change room, carrying boxes and boxes of girdles and bras. She finally came out all flustered and walked toward me.

"I'm sorry, but there is nothing we have in the store or in the catalogue that would be suitable for your mother's needs. Unfortunately, because of her weakened state, she is unable to pull up the girdles and we do not carry the wide models of brassieres that fasten in the front that your mother is looking for."

Disappointed, I thanked her for all the attention she had given Mother, while she again apologized for her earlier behaviour.

I went back to the change room and helped Mother put her coat on before we walked to other stores in the mall to see if we would have better luck. We were on our way out when I heard a voice saying, "Sir, oh sir."

I stopped and turned around to see if I was the person being addressed. It was the saleswoman walking in haste toward us with something in her hand. As she reached us, she handed me a business card and indicated that, in talking with one of her colleagues about the situation, she had learned that there was a small company in the area that would be able to help, as they specialized in such items. (By searching the subject of "Adaptive Elderly Clothing", you should find available resources.)

I thanked her for her help and we continued on to the other stores. The outcome was the same—what my mother wanted and needed was no longer available. After all this walking from store to store, Mother was a bit tired and hungry, so we went to the food court and had some lunch and a cup of tea. Afterward, we made our way to the grocery store where we got a few groceries and then headed back home. Within a few minutes of settling in her favourite chair, Mother was asleep, as the morning had certainly been full of excitement. Little did she know about some of the things that had transpired between the saleswoman and myself; I had chosen to keep those very uncomfortable minutes to myself.

I put the groceries away and while Mother rested I called the number on the card. A nice woman answered and I proceeded to tell her some of the story and asked if her organization was able to help my mother. She said that they certainly could, so I made an appointment for their representative to come over the following Saturday morning to meet my mother and discuss her needs. When Mother awoke, I told her about the call and that someone would be here the following week. She was delighted to hear that maybe she would be able to get new garments.

The week seemed to fly by. The following Saturday morning at the agreed time, the doorbell rang. It was two ladies from the company I had contacted. I invited them inside and we sat in the living room to get acquainted. After a few words about what Mother was seeking, they asked Mother if they could go with her to the bedroom to take some measurements. About forty-five minutes later, they all came out of the bedroom, saying they had what they needed to custom make the garments for Mother as well as other items she wanted.

About ten days later they called to make an appointment for a fitting. Everything fit to perfection. Mother now had a custom-made corset which was secured firmly with a downward zipper and a Velcro panel instead of lace, a wide custom-made brassiere that secured in the front, and a couple of house dresses that had Velcro closures in the front; all items were wash-and-wear. When I asked about slippers and other footwear, they recommended a store in town that specialized in such items. Mother was now all set; she now had various garments that were easy to put on, making her life easier and enhancing her independence.

Though the incident with the saleswoman had been embarrassing and insulting, it had led to a worthwhile result. Thinking about both this and the bathroom incident, I realized that nothing in the world could have prepared me for these situations. I suppose if I had been Mother's daughter instead of her son it would have been a very different outcome, but things were what they were and we had managed. As the saying goes:

"Don't worry why things happened the way they did; just let go, live and learn." – Unknown

Chapter 13
Bea's Visit

As I got my little garden patch ready for the second summer, I made a few changes based on the experiences of the first summer. Then I waited for nature to take its course. It certainly was not what I had been accustomed to, growing up on the farm; however, it met our needs.

On the farm, we had had a huge garden. There were rows upon rows of all sorts of vegetables: beans, beets, cabbages, carrots, corn, cucumbers, parsnips, peas, peppers, potatoes, tomatoes, turnips, and more. In different areas of the farm there were various kinds of wild berries. We also had a large orchard with various kinds of apples—some ripened early- to mid-summer while others were ready in the fall. With a large family like ours, it was normal to grow large quantities of all sorts of produce which could be stored, frozen, pickled, pureed, or made into some sort of jam, sauce, or relish.

Caring for such a large garden was a lot of work, but in hindsight all worth it. One of my fondest memories was going out to the garden in the morning after doing chores and getting some fresh tomatoes to eat with toast. What a delicacy! There is nothing like it. Now that I grow a lot of my own herbs, I add sweet basil or cilantro leaves to the mix. Delicious!

Ever since those days, I make a point of growing some vegetables. Some years I'd have a small tomato plant on my balcony. When I had the space, I'd have a small garden with all sorts of vegetables. In later years I discovered the "square foot" gardening method that made it possible to grow a variety of vegetables in a very small space with very little maintenance.

Since my departure from Pembroke, I telephoned Bea on a regular basis to see how she was doing. It was always a pleasure chatting with her and catching up on each other's lives. In late May, during our conversation, she talked about her two sons who were very far away and how she found it a bit lonely. I had been thinking about this and had already discussed it with Mother, so I spontaneously invited Bea to come and spend some time with Mother and me. It would be nice for her to do something different and also a great opportunity for Mother and Bea to meet face-to-face after all this time of talking on the phone. She accepted my offer. I sent her a letter with all the directions.

Once we settled on the date of her arrival, I made arrangements with my boss to take a few days of vacation so that I could make plans for a small trip in the area. Bea would be arriving on a Thursday in mid-July, spending a few days, then going back on the following

Monday as she had to be back for a doctor's appointment. In preparation for her visit, I went to the tourism office not far from work to see what was going on during that time in Ottawa and the region. There was plenty to do, so much so that it was difficult to decide.

Besides, I did want Mother, Bea, and I to take some time to sit and chat at the house on the deck, depending on the weather. A few weeks earlier, I had purchased and installed a very large canopy that covered most of the deck. Now we could sit in the shade and enjoy the backyard, which by now had changed quite a bit.

My various planned projects continued. The major one was to transform the piles of soil and gravel into a beautiful flower garden. Weekends were dedicated to the task. The first thing was to use a wheelbarrow to move the piles of gravel to a place in the back that was wet because of a dip in the terrain. Then I could move some of the soil to create a more level area that could be seeded with grass, with a gentle slope towards the forest to ensure drainage. While moving the gravel, I discovered a buried concrete slab about 6 metres (about 20 feet) in diameter. This was a total surprise. I figured that eventually it would be a great location for the planned gazebo.

Mother had always loved to have flowers in and around the house so, with the help of my brother-in-law and his two sons, we built a flowerbed along the property where I put the rest of the soil plus another truckload I had delivered. I planted all sorts of flowers—both annuals and perennials, including several varieties of daisies, which were Mother's favourite. I even had some moonflowers, which came in white and pastel colours.

These flowers would reflect the brightness of the moon, creating a spectacular view on moonlit evenings.

On the deck, there were several planters in the corners plus some boxes on the railing. I had petunias, geraniums, pansies, dracaenas, and other varieties that Mother especially liked. Throughout the years we lived there, I always had flowers in the house. In the spring and summer, there were daffodils and tulips, lilacs and other spring blooms, black-eyed Susans and white daisies, and multi-coloured gladiolas. In the fall I always had some of the hydrangeas that turned pink and light brown and would make a beautiful dried arrangement throughout the winter.

June flew by and in no time at all we were but a few days before Bea was to arrive. The night before, I called to confirm. She said she was already packed and would be arriving mid-afternoon. By then I had narrowed down all the possibilities for a day excursion to two. The first was a visit to the Museum of Civilization (now called the Museum of History) where there was an exhibition of ancient artefacts as well as a complete showcase of one-of-a-kind kimonos; the other was a picturesque ride aboard the Hull-Chelsea-Wakefield steam train, which ran along the Gatineau River. (Unfortunately, this train is no longer operating.) Thinking that either of those two options might be something interesting for all three of us to do, I got all the necessary information I needed to talk about them after Bea had settled in.

Bea arrived safe and sound in her little red pickup truck. As soon as she drove in, I went outside to greet her. We hugged and exchanged a few words about her trip; then we went inside for her to meet Mother. We all sat in the living room and chatted about all sorts of things over some tea and cookies Bea had brought. She was very clear about the fact that the cookies had no sugar but instead used apple juice as a sweetener.

We sat outside and had great conversations about a variety of topics. I talked about a few things we could do during her visit and we settled on the steam train excursion. When it came to mealtime, I slipped away and left them together to continue chatting.

Evenings were mainly spent in the living room, Mother talking about her life on the farm and Bea sharing some of her family history, even some of the very personal things that she rarely shared.

On the day of the excursion, we had an early breakfast and made our way to the steam-train station as the daily departure was at 10:00 a.m. We settled in and soon after we were on our way. The train meandered slowly through the city and headed toward the Gatineau River. It followed the river at a pleasurable pace, giving all onboard ample time to admire the site—the flowing river, the picturesque mountains, the farms and beautiful homes popping up here and there.

Aboard the train there was some entertainment— young men and women who sang, played various string instruments, and did magic tricks for the kids. There was also someone that came through to sell beverages and snacks. It was a very enjoyable trip, which lasted about an hour.

Upon arrival in Wakefield, we disembarked and were led to an area where we were able to observe the steam locomotive making its way to an old-style roundhouse turntable. There the engineer and his assistant turned the locomotive around so that it could then take a secondary track and make its way to the back of the train which would then become the front for the return trip. It was surprising to see a massive locomotive teetering on the tracks on this very large turntable being turned 180 degrees with only the strength of the two men. This demonstration was definitely something from the heydays of train travel.

We had a couple of hours to visit the village of Wakefield, going to a small café to get some lunch and then going to some of the small country-style shops which sold various items made by local artisans. We rested every now and then on the benches located in the village. The train whistle blew several times about fifteen minutes before the scheduled return trip, to remind the travellers to come back and board the train.

The return trip was as enjoyable. In all it was a very interesting and certainly different day for all three of us. Mother and Bea talked about it the whole drive home and well into the evening. By about eight o'clock both retired to their bedrooms as it had been an exhausting day.

I retired to my quarters and reflected on the day. I was very glad that I had been able to arrange this excursion and that both my mother and my adoptive mother, figuratively speaking, had enjoyed it as well. The next day after lunch, Bea got back on the road to head back home. It had been a great visit for all of us.

"Good friends are like stars. You don't always see them, but you know they're always there!" – Unknown

Chapter 14
The Cookie Enigma

It was now September, almost two years after Mother had moved in with me. At my workplace, fall also meant time to go back on the road. At the end of the month, I was scheduled to deliver several courses at the training facility that was owned and operated by my organization. The college was about an hour-and-a-half east of Ottawa and about 40 minutes from Montreal. I was to be away for three days. I said my goodbyes to Mother on Sunday evening as I would be leaving quite early on Monday morning. I would call her every night after dinner to make sure everything was fine.

On the Wednesday, I was in class lecturing. Around mid-morning, right after the coffee break, someone knocked at the door and signalled for me to come out. I was informed that they had received a call from someone named Donna, saying that my mother had been discovered unconscious earlier that morning. She had been taken by ambulance to Ottawa General Hospital.

I immediately rushed back into the classroom and asked my colleague to take over as I had a family emergency. I apologized to the participants and quickly got my things and got on the road. Sooner than I wish to admit to, I was back in Ottawa at the hospital. Upon my arrival, I inquired as to Mother's location. I went to the nurse's station on her floor and asked about Mother's condition.

According to what they knew, it would seem that, when Donna had arrived in the morning, she had found Mother on the kitchen floor, unconscious. She had immediately called 911. The ambulance arrived shortly thereafter and Mother was rushed to the hospital's emergency care unit.

Based on the assessment made upon her admittance, the probable cause for her loss of consciousness was due to an extremely high blood sugar level. She had been put on some sort of intravenous to lower her blood sugar count. She had awakened some time later, confused and lost. Further tests had been done to determine if there were other causes. Results of these tests were expected to be available later in the afternoon.

I was led to the room where Mother rested. The nurse prepared me for what I was going to see. Mother had hurt herself when she had fallen. They had taken some X-rays and found no broken bones. When I entered the room and walked around her bed, I was totally shocked. Her face and forehead were all black and blue and swollen. I could not believe what I saw. She was very still. The nurse told me that they had given her a sedative to help her sleep and rest. I stayed a little while by her side, holding her hand.

Shortly after, I called my brothers and sisters to inform them of the situation. They were all surprised and asked about how all this happened; however, I had no answers. Those would come after Mother had rested and would be able to tell me what had occurred.

In the meantime, I went back to the room and stayed with her into the night. She regained consciousness slightly, asking for water. Around eleven, the nursing staff suggested I go home and get some rest. The doctor would be in a better position to make an evaluation of the situation based on the results of the different tests.

I arrived home some time after midnight. I knew that I would not be able to sleep, so I decided to put on some quiet music and make myself a cup of tea. I put the water on to boil while I changed out of my work clothes. By the time I came back to the kitchen the water had boiled. I took a tea bag out of the cupboard and put it in the cup with the hot water. I was putting the tea bag wrapper in the garbage when I noticed an empty bag of chocolate chip cookies.

I had bought those on the weekend and had hidden them because it was not wise for Mother to eat something so very high in sugar. I had eaten a few but certainly had not finished the bag. I wondered if Mother had found the cookies and eaten them, which would probably be the cause of her losing consciousness. I would have to investigate the next day in order to get to the bottom of this mystery.

The following day, I called Donna before she left for work as she usually went to another home before coming to ours. She told me that she had arrived as usual, at around 10:00 a.m., calling out a greeting as she usually did when she came in. There had been no answer. She walked into the kitchen and found Mother lying on the floor near the table. She checked to see if she was breathing. Upon confirming this fact, she called 911 for help. She had put a pillow under her head and covered her with a blanket until the paramedics had arrived to take her to the hospital. Before leaving, Donna cleaned up the dishes. She said that the empty cookie bag was on the kitchen counter. I thanked her for everything and assured her that I would call back once I knew more about Mother's condition.

I made my way to the hospital to see if I could get more information. When I got to Mother's room, the doctor was still there. I went over to the bed, wanting to speak to Mother.

"Maman, comment ça va?"

She did not recognize me. She was awake but still sedated. The doctor moved closer to me and asked if I was Jean-François. I shook his hand, asking him how he knew my name. He said that Mother had asked for me earlier in the morning. I asked him if he had any idea what had happened to Mother. He took me aside, and told me that, based on test results, Mother had lost consciousness after ingesting something that was extremely high in sugar, and this over a short period of time.

My reaction was immediate. "The cookies!" The doctor looked at me a bit puzzled. "Cookies?"

"Yes," I said, "When I got home last night, I noticed an empty bag of chocolate chip cookies in the trash. I had bought those on the weekend and put them out of Mother's sight. I wondered if that might be the cause, so the next morning I called Mother's caregiver. She confirmed that she had found an empty cookie bag on the kitchen counter. I concluded that Mother had found them and eaten the entire bag."

The doctor agreed with me that if she had indeed eaten the entire contents of the bag, then that might have been enough to create the condition that ended in her losing consciousness. I spent the morning at Mother's bedside.

By mid-afternoon she was talking a little. She was quite confused and lost. Holding her hand, I tried to calm her as best as I could.

Over the next few days, I spent many hours at her side, reassuring her that everything would be fine and she would be back on her feet in no time. Over the course of these few days, with the help of the doctor we were able to put the pieces together. She had indeed eaten the entire bag of cookies. She had felt lonely, and, in going through the cupboards, had discovered the cookies, which she proceeded to eat for breakfast.

After Mother had spent a few weeks in the hospital, I was informed that she would have to be moved to a care facility. Medically, there was nothing more they could do. After this terrible ordeal and because of her weakened state, she now needed a lot of rest. Unfortunately, she could not come home right away, as her mobility was non-existent. Her worst fear would become reality—she had always dreaded having to live in a nursing home. She equated that to a death sentence.

Explaining the move to her would be difficult. I would enlist the support of social services and the doctor to be able to convey the short-term need to go into a care facility until she had regained her strength and could come back home. I was not looking forward to having this conversation with Mother.

Chapter 15
Christmas Surprise

The conversation about going to a nursing facility did not go badly. Though she understood very clearly that her independence was extremely limited, Mother certainly voiced her displeasure. However, the doctor and I had reassured her that it would be temporary. As soon as she could walk on her own and regain her mobility, she could come back home.

It took a week to ten days before a suitable place was found and arrangements could be made to move Mother. My sister and I went around the area to visit a number of facilities. Our first objective was to find a place that was clean, bright, and well managed. Secondly, it had to have the capacity to take Mother within a very short time frame. It was mid-October and the fall foliage was in full force. We spent the better part of a couple of weekends touring a half dozen or so places with which we had made prior arrangements to visit.

It did not take long for us to determine the telltale signs of facilities that were well managed and those that were not. First, there was the outside: some had well-planned and clean areas for the more mobile patients to sit and enjoy nature, while others had either dilapidated surroundings that showed multiple signs of neglect, with broken furniture and uneven pathways; some places had nothing at all that would allow for a short walk outside or even a place to sit.

Second, there were the smells one encountered while visiting the main room, eating area, and patient rooms. In some care facilities, one was bombarded with strong smells of greasy food, moisture, and even urine, while in other facilities there was a fresh, almost spring-like smell wherever we went.

Another indicator we observed was the behaviour and attitude of the personnel who worked in these institutions. It seemed directly related to the smells. If the facility was clean, then individuals were attentive, joyful, smiling, and most courteous. However, in other places, individuals were gloomy, somewhat rude, and rough in their behaviours and actions with patients and with us.

We eventually found a lovely place in Limoges, about 40 kilometres (about 25 miles) east of Ottawa and they could take Mother on short notice. It would prove to be the right choice as it was only a 20-minute drive from where we lived. The patient care was exceptional, many of the nurses were bilingual, and they were very helpful. They even served us a variety of healthy snacks with a beverage so that we could taste firsthand the freshness of the food.

Arrangements were made with the ambulance service to transport Mother to the care facility. Upon her arrival, I was there to greet her. The social services counsellor had explained that a familiar face would make the transition easier for Mother. I introduced her to the head nurse and some of the other nurses who would be caring for her. Mother was pleasant but was quite evidently sad that she was going to be living there. She sat in a wheelchair as they gave her a tour of the entire centre. Because we had arrived in the late afternoon, I was asked to stay and have dinner in the dining area with her and the other residents.

Mother chatted with some of them. After dinner, I took her back to her room and helped her into bed. After we talked for a while, she began to doze off, so I said my goodbyes and told her I would be back the next day.

Over the coming weeks, Mother became more accustomed to her new environment. I would usually go and spend an hour or so with her after work, except on days when I was away on business. My siblings would try to come and see her once in a while; however, they had a long distance to travel.

Many times during our evening chats, Mother would ask me when she could come home. It was still not possible for her to come back home as she could not yet get around by herself. The nurses would help her sit in a wheelchair and take her to the sitting area or the dining room. She was gaining strength but at a slow pace. The request came often, but I no longer knew what to respond as the doctor and the nursing staff could not see enough improvement to let her come home.

One evening, I called a friend to catch up on some news. We were colleagues when I lived in the Pembroke area and we had become good friends. She had worked many years with the elderly and I thought she might be able to give me some ideas on how to deal with the situation.

When I explained my dilemma, she suggested that I discuss the issue with Mother honestly yet calmly. Calling on her experience, she shared the idea of giving Mother a goal to achieve—something for her to work toward that would result in her coming back home. I spent the following days thinking about all sorts of things that might be both realistic and workable.

Mother had been in the care facility for a number of weeks now and December was only a few days away. Two or three days later, I left work and drove directly to the care facility to see Mother instead of having dinner first, as I usually did. When I arrived, a nurse was coming out of the dining room with Mother in a wheelchair to take her back to her room, so I offered to do that for her. She thanked me as they had several patients who needed to be taken back to their rooms after dinner and sometimes the last ones might have to wait 15 to 20 minutes before they could go back to their rooms. As I took Mother to her room, I suddenly remembered something the doctor had said: "You can go home as soon as you are mobile."

Back in her room, Mother and I chatted about the day's events. Of course, the usual question about when she could come home came up. But this time I had an answer. We talked about the time before she became ill and how she got around the house on her own and was quite independent. She agreed that that was a wonderful time. We also talked about the present and how she was still unable to walk very far. This too she agreed was the challenge.

I reminded her what the doctor at the hospital had said and proposed that once she could walk to and from the dining room with or without a cane, and without a wheelchair or someone to hold her, then she would be ready to come back home.

She looked at me and was silent for a few moments. Then she said, "Oui, je suis capable de faire cela."

She agreed that she would work at it every day, at first walking part of the way with the help of a nurse until her strength and balance allowed her to walk all the way by herself to the dining room and back.

Mobility was the key. For Mother to continue to be comfortable in our home, she had to be able to get around by herself. Over the coming weeks, she continued on her road toward her goal. Every evening she would tell me—and sometimes insisted on showing me—how far she had made it that day. Not only were her strength and ability to get around improving, but also her spirit and *joie de vivre* were increasing.

Three days before Christmas, I had still not made any plans or started any decorations inside or outside the house as I had been away for a few days for work. I had flown in the late afternoon, picked up my luggage, and made my way to my car, driving directly to see Mother.

Upon arriving at the nursing home, I said hello to the nurse at the reception area. She looked at me, gave me a big smile and two thumbs up. Right then and there I knew that Mother had been successful. The nurse indicated that today had been the second day in a row that Mother had made it to the dining room and back all on her own.

When I walked into her room she was sitting with her eyes closed, so I said, "Bonsoir, Maman, c'est Jean-François," and waited for her reaction. She slowly opened her eyes and, moving her head in a circular motion to figure out who was in the room, she smiled in a way I had not seen in a long while saying, "J'ai réussi, j'ai réussi!

She proceeded to tell me that for the past two days she had been going to the dining room for all her meals on her own and she was even going to the sitting room to chat with some of the other ladies during the day. Then she said, "Can I come home now?"

I laughed. Then I sat down next to her, took her hand in mine and said, "Of course, but I have to get the house warm and ready for you. I have been away, so I will get everything ready tomorrow, Friday, and I will come and get you Saturday morning after breakfast. Is that okay?"

She was a little disappointed; I guess she was hoping to come home that instant. However, the house needed warming up and I had so many things to do to get everything ready.

"OK, ça ira pour samedi matin, she said reluctantly.

We chatted for a while about how she had accomplished her goal with the help of the nurses. She was very happy. I had not seen Mother like this in many weeks. Before leaving that evening, I spoke with the nurse on duty and made arrangements for picking up Mother on Saturday morning. The nursing staff knew that Mother had been working toward this goal and they had been extremely accommodating in helping her get her strength back. I knew that had taken more of their time. I would have to find a way to thank them.

The next day I called my boss and explained what had happened. I asked if I could take the day off as well as the few days between Christmas and New Year's. She willingly agreed, given that I had put in a lot of time for work in the past months.

As soon as I was off the phone, I called my sisters and brothers to tell them the good news. The reaction from some of them was surprising—one of them expressed surprise that she was coming home, since she had been doing so well in the nursing facility. This is when I realized that the expectation from the get-go was still alive— that Mother should be in a home. For me the issue was closed: Mother was able to move around, she had most of her mobility back, and she was coming back home.

I spent the entire day getting the house ready for Mother's arrival. The first task was to get the temperature up; the second was to decorate the entire house for Christmas. Not too far from where we lived there was a place where you could cut down your own tree, so I did that. On the way back, I stopped at the grocery store to get various items to replenish the refrigerator as well as things for a Christmas Day meal.

I decorated the fireplace mantle, put a Christmas tree in the living-room, decorated with multi-coloured lights and ornaments. I even put a few lights outside. At the front of the house, on each side of the door there were globe-shaped cedars on which I put green and blue lights. I got the fireplace all ready with kindling and dry pieces of wood, so I could start it before leaving in the morning. Once all this was done, I did a thorough cleaning of the entire house. It was sparkling clean, warm, and ready for Mother's return.

On Saturday morning after breakfast, I started a small fire in the fireplace, making sure the screen doors were closed, turned on a few lamps, and went to pick up Mother. I arrived around ten o'clock. Mother was all ready to go. I signed a few papers to close the file, thanking the staff for all their help and support and wishing them a Merry Christmas. I loaded Mother's things in the car, helped her into the passenger seat, and we were on our way back home.

On the trip home, Mother was very animated as she talked and talked about her anticipation of going home now becoming a reality. When we arrived, I helped Mother inside, put her coat in the hallway closet, and walked her into the living room where she sat down in her favourite chair facing the fireplace. I stoked the fire and added another piece. She was finally back home. She was amazed at all the Christmas decorations.

I made some tea and we sat for a while, looking at the fire and the decorations while listening to soft music— neither of us saying very much. She was quite happy to be back in her home. After a few minutes, she dozed off, so I got up to make lunch, letting her rest for a while.

About forty-five minutes later I came back to get her and she was sleeping soundly, so I let her sleep. She sat there in front of the fireplace for over two hours. Eventually, she called out for me, so I came over as she was getting up and coming to the kitchen. She looked at me said, "J'ai faim." She was hungry, which was a good sign.

Due to the circumstances surrounding Mother's illness and her quick return home, I had not organized a family gathering, which turned out for the best. Having everyone here would have been too much for her as she needed some time to recuperate, get her strength and her bearing back.

We spent the Christmas holidays together, reminiscing about the past and wondering about the future. The entire ordeal had been very difficult for Mother and had unfortunately brought to the forefront her fears of having to live in a nursing home permanently. What mattered now was she was back at home and we would deal with the future as it unfolded.

Between Christmas and New Year's, Mother settled back into her routine, managing her medication by herself and moving about the house as if nothing had happened, though she moved somewhat more slowly than before. During that time, I called Donna and the VON to confirm that Mother was now back and they could come back to the house after New Year's Day to continue providing the support services. About mid-week I went out to do some errands to replenish the various food items that I needed for Mother's comfort.

In an attempt to have cookies in the house that Mother could eat, I looked in her own recipe books, which dated back to 1915, probably from her mother. There, I found an oatmeal cookie recipe in Mother's handwriting. I simply adapted it to use a sweetener instead of sugar and replaced the raisins with pecans.

Oats and Pecan Low Sugar Cookies
Makes 12-15 cookies

Ingredients

1	cup all-purpose flour (or ½ all-purpose and ½ whole wheat)
1	tsp. baking powder
½	tsp. cinnamon
¼	tsp. salt
½	cup light margarine
½	cup mixture of brown sugar blended with sweetener (available already pre-mixed in stores)
1	egg
½	cup unsweetened applesauce (or flavoured with other fruits)
1¼	cups quick cooking oats
½	cup chopped pecans (or walnuts)

Preparation

1. Preheat oven to 375° F.

2. In a small bowl, mix together the flour, baking powder, cinnamon, and salt. Set aside.

3. In a medium bowl, cream together the margarine with blended brown sugar. Add the lightly beaten egg and blend together with applesauce.

4. *Add the flour mixture and stir until well blended. Do not over-mix.*

5. *Add the oats and pecans and mix together.*

6. *Drop spoonfuls onto an ungreased cookie sheet and bake for 13-15 minutes. Makes about 12-15 cookies.*

Almost every day after Mother's return, she would talk about how pleasant and encouraging all the staff at the nursing home had been toward her. I decided to do something special to show our appreciation. Later that week, I dropped off a large bouquet of flowers and a box of chocolates to thank them for their kindness. They were surprised yet very appreciative of the gesture as, most often, when people left the nursing home, it was under very different circumstances and very few family members came back to express their thanks.

"Appreciate good people. They are hard to come by."
– Unknown

Chapter 16
Death in the family

Over the following weeks, everything went very well as the previous support services got back on track. Mother's stay at the nursing home had had at least one major benefit—the sores on her legs were completely healed. Though the healing process had started before this entire unfortunate situation unfolded, the regularity of medical attention to her legs had resulted in a complete healing of the lesions. This major improvement increased Mother's mobility and reduced the visits of the nurse to about once a month. As for the home care service, Donna came daily, arriving mid-morning and leaving mid-afternoon in order to help Mother with all her needs as well as giving Mother someone with someone she could interact with about various subjects.

Winter went by with no major incidents. Of course there was a lot of snow and many cold temperatures, but the house was quite comfortable since all the windows had been replaced with energy efficient ones. Every two months, Mother came with me into town in the morning to go to the clinic for blood work, after which I would take her back home before heading to work, usually before Donna arrived for her daily visit. A couple of weeks later we would see her doctor to get the results and make sure everything was all right. During this time, I also did a bit of travelling for work but rarely for more than a day or two.

Regularly, Mother would call everyone to get news on how things were going, especially with my brother-in-law John to get news on Josée's condition. My sister had been ill for several years now, fighting breast cancer, which had unfortunately been diagnosed very late. Though she had undergone various treatments, the cancer had spread to other parts of her body. Though Josée and the rest of the family had chosen not to provide too many details about her illness to mother, I always had a feeling that mother knew.

A few family members would call, but it seemed like Mother was the one initiating the calls most of the time. I have to say, though, that a couple of her grandchildren, Elisabeth and Sylvie, kept in regular contact with Mother, something she really appreciated and would recognize later.

Soon after Mother moved in with me, and during times when I was away from the house for several days, I would sometimes get some sort of a feeling involving Mother. At first I could not explain it, understand it, or do anything about it. However, after maybe four or five of these unusual sensations, upon my return home from one trip, I asked Mother if anything unusual had happened while I had been away.

She then proceeded to tell me that a couple of days prior, which was when I had experienced the strange feeling, she was retrieving her toast from the toaster oven when she hit her head on the cupboard door, which she had forgotten to close. The incident had been quite painful and her head had bled. However, Donna had arrived shortly after and had cleaned the wound and put on a small bandage. As she was telling me the story, I was somewhat stunned and amazed at the possibility that somehow I had felt something was wrong but could not clearly figure out what it was, except for the fact that it involved Mother.

Could it be possible that I could sense when something was not right with Mother, such as when she was experiencing some discomfort or pain? I shared with Mother what I had felt on that same morning. She was a bit surprised and even wondered if it was at all possible for me to have these experiences.

We continued to talk about other events over the previous months when I had sensed something. Some of them she recalled. It was as if we had some sort of psychic connection or bond that permitted me to feel some of Mother's emotions, be they difficult, painful, or even joyful.

Though I remembered only three or four of these premonitions or feelings in the previous two years or so, I decided that going forward I would pay more attention and follow up by calling home to speak with Donna or Mother herself to determine what was happening. I also tried to limit my travelling to the essential, engaging some of my colleagues to take on some of the projects that required being away for several days at a time.

In late March, I was asked to assess and determine a course of action concerning a conflict situation in one of the offices in the country's eastern region, something I could not delegate to one of my colleagues. Due to the magnitude of the situation, the unusual behaviours of the people implicated as well as the impact on the rest of the team, I planned to be there for nearly two weeks.

This would give me enough time to interview those directly involved in the conflict as well as all those indirectly involved but privy to the actions and the behaviours that had a negative impact on the work environment, including morale and performance. Given the number of people involved, these interviews would take a week or more, after which I would need to analyze the information, formulate a course of action, discuss it with the management team, and—once there was agreement—begin a process.

As I gathered as much information as possible, I started to get a clear picture of the turn of events that had led to this conflict situation. Friday morning, as I was completing my analysis and formulating a proposal for management, a very unusual feeling came over me. In my mind's eye, I saw Mother unconscious on the floor of the kitchen back at home.

I immediately went to the phone and called home. Donna answered on the second ring as she normally did and there was no sense of panic in her voice. I asked her how things were and if she was still able to drop in on the weekend as we had agreed. She responded that, yes, she would come by and make sure Mother was fine. She then passed the phone over to Mother and we chatted about her week and how my work was going.

From our conversation, it seemed there was nothing unusual happening. After a brief exchange we said our goodbyes. I stood there somewhat confused, looking at the phone and wondering what I had experienced. Was it possible that I was imagining things or was what I saw something to come rather then something that was happening? During the rest of the morning, I struggled to finish what I was working on as my mind kept going back to my earlier experience. Around lunchtime, I finished my proposal, printed a few copies for the afternoon meeting and went to get a bite to eat.

Walking back to the office, I decided that I would discuss with the general manager the possibility of going home that night and coming back on Sunday in order to be on the job first thing Monday morning. The debrief meeting went well and there was agreement on the course of action to address the situation. My leaving that evening was not an issue, as he had not expected that I would stay over the weekend anyway. After the meeting I changed my travel arrangements and flew back home.

Around 8:00 that evening I arrived home, much to Mother's surprise as she was preparing for bed. I did not talk about what I had felt but said that after the week I had experienced, I needed to get away for a few days. I called Donna to let her know I was back and that she did not have to drop by on the weekend, thanking her for her flexibility. Mother and I talked for about an hour, after which we both retired to our respective rooms. It was past Mother's usual bedtime and it had been a tiring week for me, ending on a strange note.

The next morning, I was awakened around 7:30 by the phone. It was my brother-in-law, telling me that my sister Josée had passed away. Though most of us knew this ending was inevitable, it was still a shock to hear it was now over. John and I talked for a few minutes and he said that he or one of his children would get back to us with more details.

I got dressed and went upstairs to the kitchen. I knew I now had to announce this sad news to Mother. Shortly after, she walked into the kitchen where I was preparing breakfast, asking who had called. I walked toward her to have her sit, but she looked at me and said, "Josée is dead, isn't she?" I barely had time to say yes before she lost consciousness. Because we were close to each other, I was able to catch her before she hit the floor. I gently carried her to the sofa in the living room to give her time to recover her senses.

This is what I had seen in my mind's eye, an event that was to come and would have happened had I not come home the previous evening. She would have gotten up to answer the phone and would have spoken directly with John. As I returned to the living room with a glass of water, Mother started to stir slightly and opened her eyes.

"Maman, est-ce que ça va?"

She said nothing for a few seconds and then said, "Est-elle vraiment décédée?"

"Yes, she is. The phone call was from John letting us know that Josée had passed away a few hours ago at the hospital. She had been admitted several days earlier because the pain had become intolerable for her to bear." The date was April 1ˢᵗ, 1995, a day we would all remember for years to come.

Mother broke down in tears. "I hope she did not suffer too much."

Josée was not only her first-born but also the second child she had lost to an illness.

Over the weekend, information concerning the funeral arrangements was communicated to everyone. Given the situation, I did not go back to my assignment, informing my boss and the manager that I would be off for the next week.

We discussed what we would do. Considering the sadness she was experiencing, her minimal eyesight, and the stress of going the day before to the funeral home, we decided that it would be best to drive down the morning of the funeral and go directly to the church service.

I certainly could understand her position, so I called John and then my siblings to inform them of when Mother and I would be arriving. The funeral day arrived and we were on the road quite early in order to be able to manage any unforeseen situations along the way and to be there for eleven o'clock.

As usual, we would stop for a short rest every hour or so to stretch our legs. The drive down was silent at times and quite animated during other times as we both recollected past memories and events involving Josée—some sad and others funny.

A couple of blocks from the church, we stopped for a few minutes, as mother was not feeling well. There was a small diner nearby, so we stopped there for a few minutes. Mother went to the ladies' room and was there for quite a while. She came out, somewhat pale and weak. The stress and the pressure of the whole situation were causing a lot of discomfort. We got back into the car and drove to the church. We were among the last ones to arrive before the service began. We were brought in to sit behind John and the two kids.

As we sat there, a man dressed in black came in carrying an urn containing my sister's ashes. He placed it on a table near the altar. The service was simple yet touching. Many people could be heard sobbing, including most of the family. After the service, we went down to the basement to chat with everyone present, offer condolences, and reminisce about Josée and how she had touched our lives in so many ways.

I suggested to Mother to sit down and have something to eat, she did sit; however, she declined to eat anything, afraid that she might experience more discomfort. About an hour after the service and after exchanging words with everyone, Mother asked that we be on our way. She was finding the interaction with so many people very difficult and tiring, so I went around to family members to let them know we were leaving. My brother invited us to stay the night, but Mother wanted to go back home and grieve by herself.

The trip back home was very quiet, except for the occasional memory that would come to Mother—"Do you remember when Josée…?" She did not even want to stop to eat and we only stopped once for a bathroom break. We were home by early evening. As Mother went to change into her nightgown, I prepared a bit of dinner. Though she sat with me, she ate very little. Suddenly, she looked at me and said; "I did not see the casket, so I don't think Josée is gone."

At first I was shocked by what she had said, then realized that with her reduced vision, she probably did not see the urn. I explained to her that there was no casket as Josée had expressed her wish to be cremated. Instead, there was an urn on a small table at the front of the church and with all the excitement, her personal discomfort, and the stress of losing her eldest daughter, she had not paid attention to what was happening in that area of the church.

Over the weeks that followed, Mother would often sit by herself in the living room, saying very little. I tried to cheer her up in any way I could but with very little success. On occasion she would say, "C'est pas correct, un enfant ne devrait pas mourir avant sa mère."

For Mother, losing a child was unacceptable, especially given that this was the second child she had lost.

Though I had to go off to finish the process I had started, I tried to limit my travel. Donna's compassion and support were phenomenal. She came every day during the week, sometimes arriving earlier or leaving later than expected.

She often came to see Mother during the weekend, sitting with her, holding her hand, talking with her, and listening to her stories. Sometimes they would go into the hallway where there were pictures of all Mother's children and grandchildren. There, Mother would reminisce about some past events and when she came to Josée's picture, she would shed tears.

As the weeks passed, she continued to keep in contact with everyone, especially with John and the kids. She also kept in contact with Elisabeth, whose son had been born a day or two before Josée passed away. Due to the shortness of our trip to attend the funeral, Mother had not seen her great-grandchild, something she wanted to remedy over the summer months.

During one of these conversations, John asked Mother if he could buy a headstone, one that would show that my father and Josée were buried there, and that eventually Mother would rest in peace there. Mother agreed and even offered to pay for half. After Father had passed away, Mother had decided not to place a headstone as there was already a large one there with the family name, purchased in the 1950s.

At some point, Josée had asked Mother her permission to be buried next to Father upon her death. Mother had been taken aback at the nature of her request. Not that she opposed the idea, but rather she was of the belief that Josée had many more years to live and also that she, my mother, would die before her daughter—something that would not come to pass.

Chapter 17
Blue Skies

Throughout the months that followed, our lives slowly got back to a routine. Mother continued her regular visits to the family doctor. As a general practitioner who specialized in dealing with older patients, he suggested that she have her eyes examined by a specialist to determine if something could be done to improve her eyesight. His office made an appointment with an ophthalmologist[12] in order to review Mother's situation and make a determination of some sort. This situation did raise Mother's spirits, as the possibility of her eyesight improving was certainly appealing to her. For one, she enjoyed reading—something she had not been able to do for a number of years now.

This being said, every now and then I had observed Mother looking into nothingness, showing a very sad

---

12 **Ophthalmologists** are trained to provide the full spectrum of eye care, from prescribing glasses and contact lenses to complex and delicate eye surgery. Definitions from *www.medicinenet.com*

face and quietly saying the same thing she had said after the funeral and several times after that, "It's not right; a child should never die before their parent."

The results from the examination at the ophthalmologist became a beacon of hope for Mother. Though there was some damage from the numerous strokes she had experienced years prior, there were also cataracts[13] that could be operated on. Within two weeks, she was scheduled to go for surgery on one eye. After a healing period of three to four weeks, the other eye would then be operated on.

At each scheduled date, I took Mother to the hospital and waited for her to come out of the recovery room. When the nursing staff wheeled her out, she looked like she had been in a fight; she looked extremely fatigued and had a bandage on her eye and part of her forehead. Due to the type of surgery, they had injected a numbing medication around the eye and the eye patch would have to stay on for a few days, after which we would come back to have it removed by the doctor to determine how the healing was progressing. During that time her mobility was greatly reduced.

After the removal of the bandage, I expected Mother's vision to be greatly improved but based on her reaction, there was some improvement but not as much as she or I had expected. Some time later, we went back for the surgery on the second eye, following the same steps—surgery, recovery, fatigue, an eye patch, several days of waiting, and finally the removal of the bandage. After a number of weeks had passed, the improvement

---

13 A cataract is an eye disease in which the normally clear lens of the eye becomes cloudy or opaque, causing decreased vision. There are three basic techniques, depending on the density of the lens. Sedation will vary accordingly.

was somewhat disappointing to both of us. I called the specialist's office to make an appointment to discuss the results.

After waiting another couple of weeks, we went back to get some answers. Mother and I were taken to an examination room and the ophthalmologist came in shortly after to determine what was happening. After a brief conversation with Mother, he looked surprised and even puzzled that the improvement was minimal. He asked Mother to relax while he examined each eye.

After a few minutes, he pushed his chair away from the instruments with which he was examining Mother's eyes, pulled them aside, so he could face her, and said, "The surgery did not work as well as expected." He then proceeded to explain to both of us that sometimes, following cataract surgery, some people start to have difficulties with their vision again. Their eyesight becomes blurred, which seemed to be Mother's case. However, he told us, this was not a re-growth of the cataract but rather a thickening of the back of the artificial lens capsules that were replaced during surgery.

The doctor ended his explanation by saying, "Don't worry, Lise. This situation can easily be remedied with a quick laser procedure."

Without losing a beat, he turned to the computer, looked at his schedule and then turned to Mother and said, "I can do the laser procedure[14] a week from tomorrow at 1:30 in the afternoon."

---

14 A very low energy beam used to cut structures inside the eye without any risk to the other parts of the eye. The doctor aims the laser exactly onto the posterior lens capsule in order to cut away a small circle-shaped area. Source: *www.rnib. org.uk*

I knew I would not be travelling for work, so we both said yes, even though we probably had a confused look. In order to get a better understanding of what was to come, I asked a few questions:

"How long does this procedure take?"

"About 20 minutes," he replied.

"How long will Mother need to wait for the second eye?"

"Oh I'm sorry, that's 20 minutes for both eyes," he said.

"How long will the bandages have to stay on?" I asked.

"There will be no bandages. Bring a pair of sunglasses for your mother as I will be administering some eye drops to dilate the pupils, making it difficult for her to see in the bright sunlight."

We left and made our way back to the car. As we drove back home, Mother's questions made me realize that she had not understood what had just happened as it had gone very fast, even for me. I explained to her the different details that the ophthalmologist had told us, about the thickening of the artificial lens that he had put into her eyes during the original surgery as well as explaining the next steps that she would undergo the following week.

Though it was a bit confusing, she seemed to understand, so I focused the conversation on the fact that the wait time for the laser procedure was minimal and that in a week or so, we would be back at the hospital and she could have the treatment done to both eyes and within 24 hours there would be significant improvement.

"Les deux yeux, es-tu certain?"

"Yes, Mother, I am certain. Both eyes will be done during the one appointment and after about 20 minutes you will be going home wearing your sunglasses to protect your eyes."

The week went by fast, and we were back at the hospital. We waited a few minutes in the waiting room before being taken to the room where the procedure was to be done. There the doctor sat Mother in a chair in front of the apparatus, put eye drops in her eyes, then brought the machine closer, so Mother could rest her chin on the base. He made the adjustment for one eye and there was a quick burst of light. Then he did the same on the second eye. There was very little preparation, no injections, and no bandages—just an appointment for a return visit to make sure everything was all right.

Saying goodbye, he shook my hand, gave Mother a quick peck on the cheek, asked her to put her sunglasses on, and told me that an orderly would arrive shortly with a wheelchair for Mother. Within minutes I was pushing the wheelchair out of the hospital to the parking lot and the car. As the doctor had told us, from the moment we arrived on the floor to leaving the hospital floor was only forty minutes or so.

I helped Mother into the car, took the wheelchair back to the entrance, came back to the car, and began our drive back home. As we got off the main highway to take the small country road that led to the house, I was concentrating on what was going to happen next. Would this laser procedure really work?

Suddenly, I heard Mother say, "The sky is such a lovely blue."

I looked over and realized that Mother had removed her sunglasses and was looking up ahead. Because of the direction we were heading, the sun was behind us, so there was no immediate concern. Mother had not seen colours and certainly not the sky this clearly in many years. The procedure had worked.

"Est-ce que tu vois bien, maman?" I asked.

"Yes. Both eyes are so clear; I can't believe it."

She could see the few clouds hovering about, the different shades of green in the fields, even the yellow-orange black-eyed Susans and white daisies along the side of the road. We were both very excited at the prospect of her eyes improving significantly. I asked her to put the sunglasses back on so as to not strain her eyes at least for the rest of the day.

After dropping her off, I went back to work as I had to finish some things, but on my way back home that evening I picked up a few things for dinner to celebrate this wonderful occasion. Mother had a special fondness for my chicken stir-fry, so that is what I prepared for our celebration meal, along with a small bottle of sparkling wine to toast this special occasion.

Stir-fry
Makes 3 to 4 portions

Ingredients

7-8	cups of your favourite vegetables, e.g., broccoli (1 ½ cups), cauliflower (1 ½ cups), red, yellow or orange peppers (1 ½ cups), mushrooms (1 cup), celery (½ cup), carrots (1 cup), onions (½ cup), cut, diced or sliced. Frozen vegetables, e.g., Thai style, can be used when fresh ones are out of season)
1	200 g (7 oz.) package of Gardein[15] Chick'n Strips or the same amount of cooked chicken or turkey strips
2	tbsp. vegetable oil
5-6	tbsp. of your favourite stir-fry/Asian style sauce or make your own with low-sodium soy sauce (¼ cup), orange juice (½ cup), minced garlic (1 tbsp.), and your favourite spices
2	tbsp. sesame seeds or ⅓ cup whole almonds or cashews pieces (optional)

Preparation

1. Heat oil (medium-low) in either a wok or a large deep saucepan.

2. When oil is hot, add all the vegetables and sauté until nearly cooked to your preference, i.e., soft or crunchy.

3. Add the Gardein Chick'n Strips or cooked chicken or turkey and your favourite sauce.

4. Stir in the vegetables, cover and let simmer for another few minutes or until the strips are hot.

---

15 Gardein™ is a brand name for a meat-free, low calorie and high protein products. Other brands include Yves Veggie Cuisine or Tofurky.

5. *Spoon over a bed of rice or chow mein noodles (or something similar).*

6. *Sprinkle sesame seeds, almonds, or cashews over the top and serve.*

Mother spent the days that followed the laser procedure exploring every room in the house—including my quarters downstairs—sometimes with Donna or myself, and sometimes by herself. We had been living together for two-and-a-half years and for the first time she was able to see every nook and cranny, the colour schemes of each room, and the many things from her own home that had been brought when she moved in with me.

As we were approaching the middle of summer, the exterior of the house was also an area of great interest—the deck, the flowers, and the garden. One night after I came home from work, she asked to go with me for a walk in the backyard and around the house to look at the entire property. She wanted to see everything there was to see.

All the stress and discomfort of the previous months slowly disappeared. Now she could slowly and carefully walk and enjoy the sights both inside and outside the house on the deck. Mother suggested that we go to the Eastern Townships that weekend. This would give her an opportunity to visit everyone, show off her new-found eyesight, see and hold her great-grandson, and visit the cemetery. Though it would be a few days before both Elisabeth's and Mother's birthdays, we would still have the opportunity to celebrate.

That evening I called everyone to make sure they would be around and to tell them that Mother and I would come for the day on Saturday. Everyone was delighted, given the last visit was under very trying circumstances and very short. The following day, Elisabeth called to tell us we were expected for lunch on Saturday at her father's home and that both birthdays would be celebrated. Mother was very happy, though she did not want anyone to make too much of it.

On Saturday morning we left after breakfast and headed to the Townships. Altogether, including the occasional bathroom break, it took about two-and-a-half hours. We arrived shortly after noon.

Mother was both excited and somewhat apprehensive about this visit as it had been many months since she had been there—though unwell, Josée had still been alive then. We parked in front of the house and, as we made our way to the front door, Elisabeth came out to greet us with her son in her arms.

After kissing Mother on the cheek, Elisabeth started to show and describe her baby to Mother. At that point, Mother did something that shocked Elisabeth. She started to comment on the baby's hair and his eyes. While Mother was holding the little hand and making sounds of endearment, Elisabeth looked at me with an expression of total surprise. When Mother noticed the look, she said, "Eh oui, ma chouette, ta grand-mère a une nouvelle vue sur le monde." Mother then proceeded to explain that she had received eye surgery and laser treatment since they last saw each other and that she could now see much better, though not perfectly.

We followed Elisabeth into the house and within minutes the news of Mother's newly improved eyesight was known by all present. Everyone came over to hug and kiss Mother and show their delight at the prospect of Mother's improved vision, which would greatly facilitate her day-to-day activities.

We all chatted for a while. Mother described the treatment and how, after so many years of near blindness, she had seen the different vibrant colours in the sky, in the forest, and in the yard around our house. She also expressed her happiness at her ability to see everybody at the gathering much better. We sat down at the dining table for a wonderful lunch, after which there was a cake with candles that both Mother and Elisabeth had to blow out.

After lunch, Mother sat in the living room and held Christopher, her new great-grandson. She was ecstatic, filled with joy and happiness. Throughout the afternoon, there were conversations going on among various members of the family. By around three o'clock, some of the family members had already left to go back to their usual Saturday activities. Mother got up to go to the bathroom and upon return walked toward me. I stood up, as it was clear that she wanted to speak to me.

"Do you think we could go over to the cemetery shortly and after that we can go back home? I am a bit tired and I want to go before I'm too tired."

"Certainement, maman," I replied. I got up and started to get our things together as we were more or less the last ones to leave. I had already spoken with John earlier of our intention to visit the cemetery, so he and his two kids, Elisabeth and Mark, said they would accompany us, leading the way in their car.

I helped Mother with her coat and we walked to the car where she settled in for the short drive. Before leaving she asked me to drive to the back of the house to see the lake, a sight she also had not seen in many years. We headed to the church then drove around back, following John to the cemetery. We had to leave the cars a little ways away as the gate was closed and locked except for the narrow pedestrian entrance.

I held on to Mother as we walked slowly over to the plot that belonged to our family. First, Mother looked at the larger stone with the family name, then we walked a bit to one side to the stone that John had ordered. It was made of pinkish granite. Carved on one side were a few stems of wheat, representing Father and on the other side a few long-stem roses, representing Josée. Inscribed on the stone were the names of my father and Josée with the dates of birth and death. Below those two names, and at the suggestion of Mother, was her own name with only her date of birth, as eventually she would also come to rest in this peaceful place next to her husband and daughter.

Mother and I looked at the stone for a few seconds and then, suddenly and without any warning sign, Mother fainted. I was barely able to catch her. Everyone rushed over to help. Mother opened her eyes moments later, a bit confused and lost. I asked her if she was in pain and she replied "No, I think the shock and emotions of seeing Josée's name on the stone surprised me more than I had considered. Aide-moi à me relever, Jean-François." With John's help, I got her upright. We waited for a few moments, then, at her insistence, walked back to the car.

We said our goodbyes to John, Elisabeth, and Mark, and left for home. Mother said nothing until we were about to take the main highway for Montreal. At that point she asked, "Can we stop at the gas station? I need to go to the ladies' room." I pulled in to the station and helped her to the bathroom. While waiting, I picked up a couple of teas for both of us. When she came out, I helped her into the car and we headed back home. Shortly after, I asked her if she wanted something to drink. She said a cup of tea would be nice, but there was no need to stop right away. I handed her the cup saying that I had already got one when we stopped at the gas station. She looked at me with a smile and said, "Tu penses à tout."

Having lived with Mother for such a long time, I had gotten used to her habits and I knew that a cup of tea was something she had always enjoyed in the afternoon. Not that Mother was influenced by the British tea time, but rather this had been her way of taking a few minutes to relax from her busy schedule of raising five children and caring for the entire household. The trip home was uneventful and very quiet. Mother probably did a lot of thinking about what she had experienced throughout the day. She also fell asleep for an hour or so on the last leg of our trip.

We were home by early evening. While Mother got ready for bed, I made a couple of curried tuna salad sandwiches that she particularly liked and some home-made cream of tomato soup. Dinner was quiet as both of us reflected on the day's events; we said only a few words and commenting on the beautiful tombstone and how it reflected so well both Father and Josée. That evening, Mother was in bed quite early as this had been a day filled with extreme emotions—first the seeing and holding of her latest great-grandson Christopher and then the visit to the cemetery.

Curried Tuna Salad
Makes 2 sandwiches

Ingredients

1	6 oz. (170 g) can flaked or chunk tuna in water
¼	cup chopped celery (more if you like it crunchier)
¼	cup chopped onions
½	cup low-fat mayonnaise
1	tbsp. curry powder (or 1 tbsp. of Dijon mustard instead)

Preparation

1. *Carefully open and drain the liquid from the tuna can.*

2. *Empty tuna into a medium bowl.*

3. *Add the celery and the onions and mix together.*

4. *Add the mayonnaise and the curry powder and gently mix together.*

5. *Using the bread of your choice, make two regular sandwiches or two open-faced sandwiches. For a different type of snack, fill celery sticks with the mixture. These make a nice appetizer.*

Home-Style Cream Of Tomato Soup
Makes 2-3 portions

Ingredients

1	28-oz (796-ml) can of diced tomatoes (unsalted)
¼	cup finely chopped onions
1	tsp. canola or olive oil
1	cup of milk or light cream
1	tbsp. sweetener (or sugar)

Preparation

1. In a medium saucepan, add oil and sauté the onions until they are translucent.

2. Open the can of diced tomatoes and pour the contents into the saucepan.

3. Heat the mixture, stirring in the milk and sweetener or sugar until well blended.

4. Bring to a boil, and then reduce heat to low and simmer for 10-15 minutes, stirring occasionally.

5. Serve and enjoy with your favourite sandwich.

Chapter 18
Late Summer Storm

The rest of the summer months went very well with a few impromptu family gatherings. Mother would often make comments about what she could now see. One evening after dinner, we were watching television—an experience that we now enjoyed together since prior to her regaining part of her eyesight, she would sometimes sit with me but would focus on listening rather than looking. Her limitation made it very difficult to see what was going on, even though I had purchased a larger television. Even with today's large flat screen models, I don't think she would have seen much more.

We were watching an episode of "Star Trek—The Next Generation"—a sci-fi series taking place on a spaceship far into the future. Normally I would watch it in the basement while she listened to other shows, but that night we had finished a program she liked and the series came on. I asked if she wanted to watch it with me, explaining the overall storyline of the program. Though that type of programming was not her usual choice, now that she had better vision she thought it would be interesting to watch.

Some of you reading this will undoubtedly understand the funny reaction my mother had; however, some of you may not understand what unfolded as Mother watched intently at what was happening.

This episode involved various characters and more specifically Worf, an alien from another planet. I confess that I am a fan of sci-fi programming and this series. I was totally engrossed in the drama that was unfolding when suddenly Mother said, "What's wrong with his forehead?" It took a few seconds for me to react and then I clued in to her question. I burst out laughing as she looked at me wondering why I was laughing at what was for her a perfectly logical question.

You see, Worf is a Klingon, a fictitious species that has very specific physical traits. He is very tall, has a very large forehead with ridges, and long hair tied in a ponytail.

Though I had given Mother a quick overview of the series, she had not caught on to the fact that some of the characters in the series were not human. I proceeded to explain that some of the characters wore very elaborate makeup to portray them as very different from humans. We had a good laugh about the whole thing. Of course there would be many other times where Mother would see something that was very foreign to her. I had to get used to the fact that Mother's eyesight had diminished over a few years and this was now nearly ten years later;

therefore, there were many things that she had not seen during that time. Some had been explained or talked about, but not seeing them had left quite a gap in her knowledge of the current environment.

A few weeks after that she asked if there was a library nearby where she might be able to borrow some books, especially mysteries, as she particularly liked the writings of Daphne du Maurier and Agatha Christie. I lent her a novel I was reading at the time and she found it to be a bit difficult to read due to the size of the font.

Using my computer at work, I wrote a couple of sentences using various size fonts, printed the sheet and showed it to her to determine her preferred size of font. It turned out that she could easily read font size 14 or above as long as she wore her glasses, even though they had not been used in many years. This was an important piece of information that I needed to know before locating any books.

Near my place of work there was a very large library, so I went to explore possibilities during my lunch period. I made my way to the information desk and asked where I could find books written by Mother's favourite authors or similar, explaining that they were for my mother who had some visibility limitations. I was delighted to discover that the library had a complete section of books printed in a larger-than-typical font size. Later that day I went back and up to the floor where these books were situated. There I found rows upon rows of books, fiction and nonfiction, covering a variety of topics such as romance, mysteries, history, geography, and much more. There were many books from the two authors Mother enjoyed, so I picked one of each, came back down to the registration desk, filled out the required documentation and I was on my way home.

Upon my arrival, I was thrilled to announce to Mother my discovery and gave her the two books. She had read one of the books before but not the other one. She indicated that she would still read them both, since it had been such a long time since she had read it. She quickly glanced at them and informed me that she could read them even without her glasses; however, she would wear her glasses so as not to strain her eyes needlessly. I started a few things for dinner and went downstairs to my room to change so as not to soil my working clothes with a splash of something hot or greasy. I was back up in a few minutes and found Mother sitting in her favourite chair, reading. I smiled to myself, pleased with my discovery.

As is normal for this part of the country, summer and early fall often brings showers, rainstorms, and on occasion thunderstorms. We were now in mid-September. During my drive home from work one day, the radio announcer talked about a thunderstorm warning for later that night and possibly into the early morning. It would not be the first one or the last, so I did not pay much attention to it except for making sure that windows on the west side of the house would be closed before I went to bed. The evening was mostly uneventful, with a few showers here and there. Mother went to bed at her usual hour and I went downstairs to do a bit of work on a presentation I was pulling together. Around 10:30 or so, I did my rounds making sure the windows were closed and the doors were properly locked and I went to bed.

Sometime in the middle of the night I heard Mother calling me, so I quickly got up and switched on the light on my night table. Nothing happened. I took the flashlight from the drawer and tried the switch at the base of the stairs. Still nothing. So I made my way upstairs. As I walked into Mother's bedroom, she was sitting up on the side of the bed. She was quite agitated as she had wanted to go to the bathroom, but there were no lights. I helped her up and guided her to the bathroom with the flashlight. I went to the kitchen to get another one that was in the drawer there and quickly came back. As she came out of the bathroom she said: "Il y a des éclairs et du tonnerre depuis un bon moment. J'ai voulu allez à la salle de toilette, mais il n'y avait pas d'électricité."

While I had slept, it seemed that a thunderstorm had come through with quite the light and sound show, according to Mother's account. At one point there must have been a lightning strike that possibly hit a transformer and the power went out. Luckily, I was at the house at the time of this incident and not travelling. I followed Mother to her bedroom and she went back to bed, keeping the flashlight on her night table, next to the lamp.

I went back to my bed downstairs; however, before falling asleep, I wondered what I could do to make sure this did not happen again, especially during a time when I might be away on business. I suppose the flashlight could remain there permanently. I fell asleep with that thought.

The next morning, my alarm went off at the usual time. As I turned to shut it off, I wondered how this was possible, given that we had had an electricity outage overnight. I sat there for a few seconds and remembered that my alarm clock had a battery backup that was good for several hours. That was the reason for the accuracy of the wake-up time. I went about my normal routine of getting ready for work, and getting things ready for Mother for when she got up.

Around 7:15 I left to go to work. As I drove, I started to think about what kind of lighting system I could set up in Mother's room, in the corridor, and in the bathroom that would work in the event of a blackout—something that would have a battery backup system that could provide enough light for Mother to move about safely. This would be something I would need to investigate in order to have peace of mind when I was away. Another piece to the puzzle, given that I was a heavy sleeper (I had not heard the thunder that night) was what I could set up that would permit Mother to signal me in my bedroom when she needed my help. This too I would investigate and resolve.

Over the weeks that followed, I went to various hardware stores, looking for a solution of some kind to my two challenges. Getting a way for Mother to signal me for my help was the first piece of the puzzle I was able to resolve. There was already available a wireless doorbell system for houses that did not have them. It was easily installed without having to run wires through walls.

Wireless Signal System

It consisted of a kit with two components:

- The first component was a small doorbell button, with a small battery inside exactly like the ones used at the entrance of modern homes. It was a simple matter of attaching it to Mother's night table. When the button was pushed, a signal went to the other component and it rang.

- The second component was a small box, also with a battery inside, which I attached to the lower wall next to my bed. Today's models even offer a choice of various bell tones so as not to be confused with the front and back door doorbells of the home.

For several weeks I checked everywhere I could think of for some sort of lighting system that would have a battery backup. I knew it had to exist as it was already available in commercial buildings but when I asked friends to check with their apartment building management they got nowhere. I even called several electrical companies, but what was being proposed was extremely expensive. At least for the time being I still had the flashlight solution.

One day I came home from work as usual, picked up the mail from the mailbox, went inside and chatted for a few minutes with Mother, then went to change my clothes. I came back up to see what I was going to make for dinner. I took several things from the freezer and started getting dinner ready. Being Friday[16], I decided that we could have fish with some rice and vegetables. I

---

16   Mother had been raised that Friday was a meatless day, so fish was one of the alternatives. Personally, I did not mind and besides, eating fish frequently was good for us.

quickly thawed[17] some frozen haddock, prepared some rice[18], and cooked some vegetables.

While all this was cooking, I went through my mail. Among the various pieces of mail there was my monthly statement from Sears Canada. I knew I had paid my balance the previous month, so I did not open the envelope immediately, focusing my attention on others like the electricity bill, one of my current preoccupations.

Mother and I sat down shortly after and had dinner, sharing with each other our day's events. After dinner, Mother went to put her nightgown and housecoat on while I did the dishes, getting settled in to watch a bit of television.

In those days there were several mystery-type programs and one was on Friday evening, so we settled in to watch it. I brought with me the rest of the mail I had not opened. During some of the commercials we chatted about various subjects and when we did not I went through my mail. I eventually got to the one from Sears. I opened the envelope and saw that there were a few promotional items with my statement. As I glanced at the flyers for watches, jewellery, and other items I did not need, I saw something that attracted my eye. It was, would you believe, a motion sensor light with a battery backup that would light up a dark area whenever it sensed any movement. Because there was a battery, it would work where there was no power. And the price was quite reasonable!

---

17 Mother had taught me that I could thaw individually wrapped portions of frozen fish quickly by putting them in warm water in the kitchen sink for 10-15 minutes.
18 I sometimes will use a low sodium vegetable broth or vegetable juice instead of water to cook rice. It gives the rice a wonderful flavour.

My reaction was spontaneous. "J'ai mon voyage, depuis le temps que je cherche quelque chose!"

"Looking for what?" Mother asked.

I explained that after the last power outage which had presented a challenge for her to get to the bathroom, I had been looking for some sort of light that I could install in different areas of the house that would sense her presence and come on whenever she sat up in bed, when she walked through the corridor and into the bathroom. They would also have to work whether or not there was power in the house. After weeks of searching and enquiring in various stores, here it was; it had come to me among the advertising flyers included with my monthly statement.

The next day I called the 800 number and ordered several of these lights, as the cost was quite affordable and I needed at least three to ensure Mother's safe movement between her room and the bathroom. The box arrived a few weeks later and that weekend I installed the lights that would give me peace of mind when I was away on business.

Motion Sensor Light

The model could be plugged into a wall outlet as well as having a battery backup. The first one I installed was in Mother's room over her bed, aligned with the side of the bed she got up on. This was a trickier process than anticipated. Getting the right height became the biggest challenge. I closed the blinds and turned off the ceiling light in order to give the illusion of darkness, which was a requirement for the light to work. As I stood motion-less against the wall holding the light with my hand, I had Mother lie in bed and move about, then get up to see if the light would turn on prematurely or not at all. It took several tries. I could not get it right. Mother was getting frustrated and so was I. Finally, after several attempts, I succeeded in getting the exact height where, regardless of Mother's movement in bed, the light did not turn on; however, as soon as she sat on the side of her bed, it turned on. I had found the ideal placement.

Another light was installed in the corridor, this one being at a slightly lower height than the first, and a third light in the bathroom. Those two, I installed only with the battery as energy as there were no wall outlets nearby. For those two, I made sure that I had good bat-teries at all times.

Though these devices were only used once or twice after they were installed, I had comfort in knowing that Mother could move about should there be a power outage in the middle of the night. It gave me as well as Mother peace of mind, something that was important to both of us.

Chapter 19
The Beginning of the End

Several months after the storm incident, Mother was hospitalized after suffering a stroke. As with the others before, the impact was very difficult for her. The mobility that she had lost and regained several times before was again decreased beyond the support I could provide her at home. She spent a few weeks in the hospital until I could find a care facility that could accommodate her condition and needs.

This time around, Mother would require 24/7 support and monitoring. She could no longer walk, as her strength had diminished considerably. The hospital put a lot of pressure on me to find a place for Mother as her condition was falling outside their mandate. Because time was of the essence, the care facility was able to take Mother immediately. They offered all the services required but at a substantial monthly cost. The high-rise building was situated along the river in Ottawa. Some of the elderly people who lived there had full autonomy while others, like Mother, needed various levels of support and medical care.

For those who were fully autonomous, the centre offered a full dining room with a varied and healthy menu, a smaller private dining room if they wished to have guests, several very comfortably furnished sitting rooms with a view of the gardens or the river, a well-stocked library, a screening room for movies, and various rooms for recreation activities. Along the riverside there was a beautiful sitting area. The facility was very well organized and the people who worked and managed the centre were very pleasant and professional.

Because of Mother's condition and her needs, she was situated on one of the lower floors close to the nursing stations. Mother's room was very pleasant, brightly decorated, and comfortable, with a complete washroom and a sitting area near the window that overlooked the river. At first, Mother required help with her meals as well as with her personal hygiene. After several weeks, she did get some of her strength back, and was able to eat by herself and, with the aid of a walker, go to the bathroom on her own; however, each trip took a lot of her energy.

As in past situations, I visited her daily, except for days I was away on business. The nursing staff would help Mother into a wheelchair and take her to the dining room to eat with the other residents in the building. The people I dealt with at the centre had also made it clear that I could visit Mother at any time during the day and up until nine o'clock in the evening. I was also welcome to join Mother in the dining room. I would take her to the dining room and back, thus relieving the staff of this task. On several occasions, mainly on weekends, I would have lunch or dinner with Mother, and then we would sit in the sitting room facing the river, which was her favourite spot. There we chatted about various subjects, mainly about family.

It was during those moments that I realized how I missed her presence at home. We had lived together for over three years and both of us had come to enjoy and appreciate each other's company and our conversations. My brothers and sister came a few times to visit with her, as did Donna, her faithful companion. I had retained the services of Donna to come to the house every other week to help with the household chores.

Mother spent several weeks in the care facility. During all those weeks, I always expected that Mother would ask when she could come home with me, as she had done in the past. Even though the doctor had told me that it would most likely not be possible, I still had hope that she might. Not wanting to raise her expectations, I never brought the subject up. However, she never talked about it. I think she knew that this time, the possibility of regaining her mobility—and to a certain degree her independence—was no longer feasible.

Ever since my sister had passed away, I had the feeling that Mother was slowly giving up on life, especially after we had visited the cemetery and she had seen with her own eyes the inscription on the tombstone.

During a regularly scheduled doctor visit that included various tests, he informed both of us that the damage to her heart was extensive and that she would require medical attention 24/7, something that would be very difficult to provide at home.

During the drive back to the care facility, I asked her how she felt about it. For a few seconds she said nothing; then she said, "Je m'y attendais." She had realized that this last stroke had been much worse and that her energy was greatly diminished. From the tone of her voice, I could tell she was not only disappointed but also sad about the prospect. I tried as best I could to raise her spirits, talking about how the care facility was a great place, about how kind and helpful the staff were, that I would come and see her every day after work and that we would have meals together on weekends. She agreed but not in her normal upbeat way.

Several weeks later, during one of my visits, we were sitting in her room after having had dinner together. During the meal, I had done most of the talking, which was a bit unusual as we normally had good conversations about things that had occurred during her day and mine. I asked her if she was feeling all right, as she had been relatively quiet during the meal. She looked at me and said, "I have been thinking about things since we last saw the doctor and I think I would like to move to a nursing home in Cowansville. It is very expensive here and there must be similar nursing homes back there at a more affordable price."

At first I was shocked. Many questions came to mind. Had she been unhappy with the living arrangement I had organized for the past several years? Had I not lived up to her expectations? Did she feel like I had abandoned her?

She probably noticed the perplexed look on my face. She then proceeded to explain that it was not because she did not like where she was now, nor that she did not appreciate living with me. On the contrary, she was very grateful for all the trouble I had put myself through, though for me it never was trouble but rather something I wanted to do.

Since it would not be possible for her to come back to the house, going back to a more rural setting was what she wished to do. On occasion, she had been a little homesick. This was not surprising, since she had lived there for the better part of her life. We talked about the next steps and what would need to be done to carry out her wishes.

That evening I contacted my brother Antoine to let him know of Mother's intentions. I asked him to enquire as to what services were available in the area and if Mother could be provided with the care, support, and comfort she required. After that, I called my two other siblings to let them know of Mother's wishes and that Mother would be moving back to the Eastern Townships once a suitable place was found for her.

It took a couple of days before Antoine called me back to tell me he had found a small yet very nice care facility in Dunham, a neighbouring village to where we had lived on the farm. He also informed me that, though the place was very nice, it was very sparsely furnished, as most residents tended to bring their own furniture. It was a similar type of care facility as the one she was now in, though maybe a quarter the size. Some residents were fully autonomous while others needed more specialized care.

We made plans for him to come up to the house the following weekend and pick up a few pieces of furniture and other items to make Mother's room more comfortable—things like her favourite chair, a dresser, a reading lamp, her bedspread, her clothes and personal care items, and of course all the pictures of her children, grandchildren, and great-grandchildren.

The next day I went to visit Mother and let her know that everything was organized, that Antoine had found a great place and that we would go down on the weekend. She was very pleased and even surprised at the speed at which everything had been organized.

I informed her current care facility that Mother would be leaving at the end of the month. On the last day of her stay, I came in early and had breakfast with her before we went back to her room and packed her things. I signed the final paperwork and we were off. The drive was quiet as I think Mother was feeling a bit torn about the whole idea. On the one hand, she clearly had appreciated her years with me; on the other hand, she did want to go back close to her home of fifty years.

We stopped for a couple of bathroom breaks and a bite to eat along the way and arrived at the residence in Dunham around two o'clock. While we were at the restaurant having some lunch, I called my brother to let him know where we were and the approximate time we should be arriving. He gave me specific directions, which were not very complicated as there was one main street and that was where the residence was located. I parked in the entranceway for easier access.

As I was helping Mother out of the car, my brother came out with an attendant pushing a wheelchair to help Mother inside. After a few exchanges and hugs we went inside as it was late fall and somewhat chilly. The attendant took Mother to her room. Both Antoine and I helped her up from the wheelchair and out of her coat. We then held on to her as we walked around the room in order for her to get her bearings. She quickly noticed the bedspread, her favourite chair, the reading lamp, and of course all the family pictures on the wall.

A few minutes later the administrator came over to greet Mother and welcome her to the residence. She understood that Mother had come a long distance and might be tired, so she told her that it would be fine if she wanted to rest for a while and that one of the nurses would be checking in every so often to see if she needed anything. She also explained that over the next few days she or one of her staff would be explaining the ins and outs of the residence; in the meantime, there was a call button next to the bed should she have a question or need something.

Antoine and I stayed with her for about half an hour until she asked if we could leave as she was a bit tired and wanted to take a nap after the long drive. We kissed her and left, with Antoine saying that he would be back later. Both of us left and went outside to chat for a few minutes. He indicated that he would take over from me, keeping a regular eye on Mother and making sure she would be comfortable and cared for appropriately. We hugged goodbye and I headed back to Ottawa.

At several points during the trip home I got quite emotional about leaving, trying to convince myself that this was Mother's wishes, so here she was to stay now. I would attempt to come back every other week on weekends to visit and spend some time with her. Late that evening I called my brother to ask how his return visit had been. He indicated that Mother was in good spirits; she had commented that she had enjoyed a good meal and had met other residents at dinner.

Over the weeks that followed, I called my brother several times to see how Mother was getting along in her new home. By his account, she was doing very well, as she was very talkative during his visits. He also reported that our brother Daniel had visited Mother a couple of times. I told him that I would be coming down to see Mother the following Saturday.

Chapter 20
The Last Touch

As promised, I went down on the Saturday and spent several hours with Mother. She was indeed in good spirits and quite talkative. She liked the staff, finding them to be very nice and cheery. She also talked about how she actually knew some of the other residents and, because most were either French or bilingual, it was easier to have conversations with them. She was able to get around with a walker, well enough to get to the dining room or sitting room to chat with other residents.

At lunch, I accompanied her to the dining room where we sat together, chatting with others around us. I became the centre of attention, as some residents rarely had friends or relatives visit them.

After lunch we sat in Mother's room for a while, talking about when we had lived together and the great times she had experienced. To this day—though I am sure she did not regret moving back home—I feel that she missed living with me. We even talked about what we would do at Christmas, as it was only a few weeks away. As I was getting ready to leave to drive back home, she asked me to get a wheelchair to sit in, so she could give me a tour of the facility, something I had not done when I had brought her over a few weeks prior.

A week later, I got a call at work from my brother. Mother had had another stroke and had been rushed to the hospital. Because of Mother's previous strokes and her current condition, she had been put in a medically induced coma[19]. He indicated that she would remain like that for a while and that coming down to see her was basically pointless as she would not be aware of my presence. He assured me that he would stay in touch and let me know of any developments. Though I was quite upset, my only thought was that at least all this had unfolded in a place where there was constant care and not here at the house when there might have been no one around or when I might have been away on business.

The following weeks were very difficult, for everyone in the family. Waiting for news—*any* news—seemed to take a lot out of me. It was difficult to keep my focus, regardless of what I was working on. The simplest task became too challenging to complete. Antoine called me every two or three days to give me an update. There was

---

19 In a medically induced coma, a patient receives a controlled dose of an anaesthetic to cause a temporary coma or a deep state of unconsciousness. This type of coma is used to protect the brain from swelling by reducing the metabolic rate of brain tissue as well as the cerebral blood flow. Throughout a medically induced coma, an anaesthesiologist or other physician in a critical care setting constantly monitors a patient's critical life functions. *http://www.lifelinetomodernmedicine. com/*

little to tell, as Mother was still in intensive care, though in stable condition.

The Christmas season came and went and, for the first time in many years, there was no family get-together, making this time of the year somewhat sombre. My sister and her husband had left in late October for warmer weather in Florida, so my brother kept her in the loop by telephone as events unfolded.

In early January, Mother was brought out of her coma, still very weak and paralyzed on the right side. She was no longer able to move her right leg and arm and her speech had also been affected. She understood what we said in French, but she responded in English. Her mother tongue capabilities had been affected somehow. This lasted about a week or two.

Given her condition and the need for more specialized care, she could not go back to the nursing home in Dunham. The only care facility that had available space was in another town a bit farther away. She was moved to the Farnham nursing home, which was better equipped to manage her condition. She could no longer walk or manage her personal needs.

There she spent several months. I visited her almost every week, spending two to three hours with her on either the Saturday or Sunday. I tried to be there during lunchtime, so I could help her eat. After her lunch I would gently put her in a wheelchair and take her to the sitting area. It gave her a bit of a change from spending all her days in her room, often by herself.

At the end of March, I was preparing to go away on vacation for a week. The Saturday before my departure, I went to spend a few hours with Mother. I helped her eat and we went for our regular stroll to the sitting area. After a little while we went back to her room. We chatted about various things. At one point, as I sat next to her, she extended her left arm and touched my cheek, saying, "You have to let me go now."

I interpreted her words as meaning that she was tired and that I should leave. Later, I would come to understand what she really meant.

I offered to help her back into her bed; however, instead she asked me to call for the attendant, as she needed to go to the bathroom. I did that and, as the attendant arrived, I kissed her on both cheeks and left, reminding her that I would be back in a couple of weeks. She smiled and I left.

That night I called my brother to let him know that I was leaving the following morning for a week's vacation and would return to see Mother upon my return. The next morning, I made my way to the airport and left for my vacation.

Upon my return home I noticed that I had messages on my phone. A few were from friends, but the last one was Antoine telling me that Mother had taken a turn for the worse, had to be hospitalized, and was now on morphine in a chronic care facility in Cowansville. It was April 1, 1996.

I immediately called him back and he informed me that Mother had had another stroke and had been rushed to

the hospital. Doctors had also discovered that her paralyzed leg was in bad shape and would have to be amputated. I gasped. "Non, pas ça." I asked him if they had
done that already. He told me no, that it was planned for
Tuesday or Wednesday.

That was why she was in a chronic care facility for the
time being until they could readmit her at the hospital
and perform the surgery. I then reminded him that
Mother always said that she did not want to be put on
an artificial system or to be cut up. If she was to die, it
was to be whole.

I told him that I would drive in early the next morning
to see her and talk to the doctor. The night was long and
restless. I left early the next morning, arriving around
eight o'clock or so. I went directly to the care facility,
parked my car and went in. As I arrived, an old college
friend greeted me. She had gone into nursing and was
working in the facility. My brother had called earlier
that morning to inform them of my arrival. Because she
knew me, she had watched for my arrival.

"Mary, what a surprise to see you here!" I greeted her.

"Hello, Jean-François. It has been many years. Come sit
with me," she said.

"Can we catch up a bit later? I want to see Mother."

"That is why I want to chat with you."

"What do you mean? Is she all right?"

"No."

As we sat in a quiet area, she asked when I had last seen Mother. I told her it had been a little over a week ago.

"What do you remember from that last time?" she asked.

"Well, we had a good few hours together. I helped her eat and then I took her for a stroll in the wheelchair. She was in pretty good spirits. She even caressed my cheek before I left."

Mary then took my hand and said, "Jean-François, your mother passed away a few hours ago. Given that you have a good last memory of your mother, I suggest that you not see her now. Sometimes, the pain experienced during the illness is visible after death."

I broke down sobbing. Mary continued to hold my hand. After a few minutes, I looked up and asked, "Does anyone else in my family know?"

"Yes. When your brother called to tell us you were coming, she had just passed away and he was informed. Actually, I am a bit concerned about him because my colleague told me that he said nothing and hung up."

A few minutes after the dreaded announcement, Antoine arrived. He was very pale and seemed to be in a daze. We embraced each other and cried. He informed me that he had called both our sister and brother to let them know. Andrée would fly in the next day, while he would go and get Daniel who had no means to travel on his own. Antoine also wanted to see Mother. I told him the same thing Mary had told me; however, he insisted on going to see her.

I then asked what the next steps would be. Mary directed us to the administrator's office. There I signed some papers and was asked that I contact one of the funeral homes in town in order to make arrangements. Once this was done, then to let them know as soon as possible. The funeral home would contact them and make arrangements with them to come and take Mother's body away. There would be no need for an autopsy given the circumstances of her death.

We left the office and immediately called a few funeral homes in town. The first one we called was able to take care of everything. We were invited to come over to make all the arrangements. Mother had always wished for a simple funeral. At the funeral home, the manager greeted us and invited us to his office. My brother held my hand and followed my lead. I had gone over this situation in my head countless times, so I was prepared. I signed a few papers, giving them the authority to go to the chronic care facility and pick up the body. We also discussed the type of funeral we wanted for our mother.

As to be expected, there was an attempt to get us to agree to what Mother would call "des funérailles extravagantes et exagérées," which she did not want. She often said that a funeral was not the time to impress and be flamboyant; rather, it was the time to remember the departed, reflecting on and laughing about the good times.

After that, we were taken to a room with many types of caskets, lined with various types of materials. There were also metal outer caskets in which a wooden one could be placed for preservation. When I asked my brother what he thought, he was silent, still in shock and quite sad. I chose a wooden casket made of maple, one of Mother's favourite trees, with a simple white lining. For Mother, the maple tree was a gift from nature— "A sweet sap to feed us, branches with many leaves to keep us cool in the shade and wood for keeping us warm."

As the funeral manager tried to convince us to go a different route, Mother's words came to me, "Simple, Jean-François, très simple." She had wanted a simple funeral and her wishes would be followed to the letter.

For the top of the casket, I asked for a large cushion-style arrangement of white daisies. Antoine, after having been silent for quite a while, spoke up and asked, "Why not roses?"

I responded, "Well, do you remember how Mother reacted when we came back from the fields and brought her daisies?"

"I seem to recall that she became very animated," he said.

"Yes, she did, because they were her favourite flowers."

After finalizing everything, we got into our respective cars and went to the church Mother used to attend to make the arrangements for a service on the Friday. Mother always said that a wake and funeral together should be concluded in three to five days, allowing enough time to publish in the papers, to contact family and friends, and to give people who had to travel time to make their way to pay their respects.

Upon arrival at the church, we talked to the priest to make arrangements for a funeral service the following Friday morning. He stopped us, informing us that was

Good Friday and that holding a funeral service was really not possible. He said that the funeral service could be on the Thursday or on the following Tuesday. I looked at my brother, and then looked back at the priest. I explained to him that Thursday was too soon, as people were coming from far away, and that the following Tuesday was too long. I asked why the Friday was not possible. He explained that on Good Friday there would be several services taking place throughout the day and it would be very difficult.

We talked it over for a while, and after a bit of gentle pressure he agreed that the funeral could take place at nine o'clock on Good Friday morning and that it would be a short mass instead of the regular mass in order for him to be able to carry out his other commitments. Final arrangements were made at the church. There only remained to contact various papers to publish the announcements and get on the phone to call everyone we could think of to inform them of Mother's passing and the details of the service.

The next day my other siblings arrived. On Wednesday evening, we made our way to the funeral parlour for the wake. That evening, local friends and family members came to pay their respects. On Thursday afternoon and evening, more people came. Mother had lived in the area for fifty years and we had grown up there, so we were not surprised at the number of people who came to pay their respects and offer us their condolences.

On Friday morning, two of us went to the funeral home for the closing of the casket while the others went to church about a half hour before the service to make sure everything was going according to plan.

Immediate family members were there as several were pallbearers. By 9:00 the church was full to capacity. The service went quickly, as expected, and then there was the procession to the cemetery for the interment. Most of us had been there just barely over a year before for my sister's funeral. Once we arrived there, the casket was carried by the funeral parlour staff and positioned over the family burial plot. The priest spoke a few words and the casket was lowered. Mother had now joined her beloved husband and eldest daughter. People walked by, said a few prayers and walked back silently to the community centre in the basement of the church.

As Mother had wished it, the next few hours were spent reflecting on her life, the joys she had brought everyone, all the birthdays, parties, anniversaries, weddings, and other events that were part of people's memories. The tombstone placed a year earlier for Father and Josée would now tell another story, a sort of "dénouement".

As some of the family went back to their homes—some close by and some several hours away—the siblings and some of the spouses spent the afternoon talking about Mother's life, her impact on all of us and how she had loved and contributed so much to her family.

That evening was quiet, as each of us reflected on what would happen now that Mother was no longer with us. She had always been part of our lives, the connecting link among all of us, including during her years living with me as well as the months spent in the care facilities.

"Treat your parents with loving care for you will only know their value when you see the empty chair." – Unknown

On Saturday morning after breakfast we met at my brother's home to read Mother's will. Mother had asked Elisabeth and me to be co-executors for her affairs. Mother had made some changes to her will during the years she lived with me. Because of the nature of some of the changes, I had asked her and she had agreed to go through a process of testing her mental acuity by a specialist, something that she passed with flying colours.

Though her eyesight was minimal for quite a while, her mental alertness was perfect. Prior to her leaving to go back to the Cowansville area, I convinced her to reverse some of her earlier decisions that would no doubt be controversial at one point or another. She had agreed, though we did not do a mental acuity test for the codicil she signed.

At one point as I read the will, I stopped to read the codicil with Mother's wishes. This interruption upset one of my siblings who then proceeded to read the part of the will that stipulated that one sibling was no longer entitled to any of Mother's assets. As expected, that section of the will triggered a lot of anger. Over the raised voices, I tried to explain that I had convinced Mother to change that part of her will and that the codicil said something very different.

The tone of the gathering became very aggressive with name-calling and finger-pointing. Luckily, my co-executor and niece Elisabeth intervened and was able to get everyone to calm down. The codicil was read out loud for all to hear and, even though some of Mother's wishes did not sit well with some of the immediate family members, we were able to finalize the reading.

This situation put me at odds with some family members and the relationship was severed right there and then. Hurtful and threatening words were used to describe me, something I could not easily accept and tolerate.

As the meeting was going to end abruptly, Elisabeth did make a very specific point: that should any legal action be taken, the original will—which had been validated by a lawyer and a psychologist—would stand and not the codicil, and that the offended parties would lose out. Therefore, she strongly encouraged everyone to go home, relax, and think things through, and then in a few days come back to her on what they were going to do.

A few days later Elisabeth informed me that everyone had agreed to abide by the will and the codicil. Over the coming weeks Elisabeth and I would carry out Mother's wishes. A letter itemizing some of Mother's personal things was sent to all the siblings with a request to identify items they wished to have. The response was minimal.

I then offered those items to nieces who took some of Mother's rings and other pieces of jewellery. Though the furniture was bequeathed to me, I asked if there were any pieces wanted by anyone else. A couple of pieces were requested. My brother Daniel wanted the hutch he had made for Mother and my sister asked for a mirror. When it was possible they were handed over.

Given the situation, neither Elisabeth nor I asked for remuneration for our work as executors, being convinced that we would have gotten push-back.

Contact with my brothers and sister severely diminished or ended. I was now persona non grata. Many of my nephews and nieces were instructed to have no contact with me, though some did anyway. I was on my own with basically an estranged family. I would have to fall back on a few good friends as support until all this might be resolved one day.

Chapter 21
Healing

During the years that followed I refocused my life, which had been basically centered on Mother. I continued living in the house I had bought for Mother, as I needed a place that was comfortable and familiar that I could always come home to after a day's work or my business travel. Then I started to reconnect with old friends and make new ones in order to rebuild my social life, all while pursuing my career.

My work required that I travel a lot throughout the country, so I was often away from home. During the time Mother lived with me, I had reduced my travel to only the essential and would often ask colleagues to replace me; now we shared the travel equally.

The following year, accepting that the house was really too big for one person, I sold it and move into a smaller condo in the western centre town of Ottawa, sufficiently close to work that I could use my bicycle or public transit.

I moved items and furniture that fit the smaller place and sold for next-to-nothing a lot of the excess furniture to Donna, who had taken care of Mother for so many years. Everything else basically sold at a garage sale.

I occasionally spoke with my brother Daniel to see how he was doing as well as to one nephew and one niece who still interacted with me. I had come to conclude that I had nothing to feel guilty about. I had done for my mother what I knew she wanted and that was the end of it.

This quote that I had read some years earlier helped me feel good about myself and what I had accomplished, regardless of what others may have said or thought:

"Right from the moment of our birth, we are under the care and kindness of our parents, and then later on in our life when we are oppressed by sickness and become old, we are again dependent on the kindness of others. Since at the beginning and end of our lives we are so dependent on others' kindness, how can it be in the middle that we would neglect kindness towards others?"
– Dalai Lama

In December 1999, a good friend who lived in Pennsylvania lost his partner in a tragic car accident. Understandably, he was depressed and quite distraught over the event. They had had a quarrel in the morning before going their separate ways to work and the car accident occurred that same morning. I decided to drive down and spend Christmas with him to support him in his grief.

After spending a few days helping him process the ordeal, I encouraged him to write a letter reflecting what he would have wanted to say that evening if the accident had not happened. We then went to the cemetery where he read the letter aloud. He then dug a small hole and placed the letter in it. It was difficult for him; however, I believe it helped him begin to come to terms with his loss.

As I drove back home, I reflected on what my friend had experienced, and thought about my own situation with my siblings and family. This was late December 1999 and Year 2000 was nearing with all of the doomsday scenarios expected to happen at the stroke of midnight. As expected, the media had had a field day in getting their readers all excited and panicking?

In any case, I decided that the situation between my siblings and myself had to be tackled head-on, so, instead of turning north to go home, I continued east to my hometown of Cowansville. I arrived mid-afternoon at my brother Antoine's place of employment. The entire notion of showing up unannounced was certainly scary. What might happen? Would he refuse to talk to me? Would he tell me to leave? What might he do? So many questions, no clear answers. I even considered going back home.

I mustered all my courage and energy and walked in. The fact that the receptionist was someone I knew from years before made the initial greeting easier.

She smiled and said, "Salut, Jean-François, comment vas-tu? Ça fait longtemps."

"Yes, it has been a while since we saw each other. How is everyone in your family?"

We chatted for a minute or two, then I asked her if Antoine was in.

"Of course, I'll check to see if he can see you," she responded. "Antoine, ton frère Jean-François est ici. Est-tu en mesure de le recevoir?"

She had barely finished speaking when Antoine's office door opened and he walked briskly toward me, took me in his arms and hugged me.

"Je suis tellement fier de te voir," he said.

He was genuinely happy to see me. We went back to his office where we sat and talked for over an hour, catching up on each other's lives. I explained that I was coming back from helping a friend deal with his loss and that this experience helped me realize that the rift between all of us since Mother's passing had to come to an end. I made the point that life is too short to be cut off from one's family.

Both of us shed tears at the whole unfortunate situation. He then suggested he call Daniel who lived only a short distance away to see if he would join us for dinner. He knew that Daniel and I were in contact, so there would be no issue other than his availability. Daniel was going to dialysis every other day and had limited mobility.

Antoine put the phone on speaker and called him. They chatted for a minute or so with no mention of me, then

Antoine said there was somebody next to him who wanted to say hello. Daniel was surprised and said, "Qui est-ce?" At that point I said, "Bonjour, Daniel. C'est Jean-François." He was totally taken by surprise, asking what was I doing there, and how was I doing. He said that he had called at Christmas but that I had not responded, and so on.

At that point Antoine asked him if he had plans for dinner that evening, as we were thinking of driving down to get together. We would drive to where he lived, as he did not have a car; however, his electric wheelchair would be able to take him to a restaurant nearby. He quickly said yes and suggested a place and a time to meet. I would answer all his questions during dinner. We said our goodbyes with an agreement to meet later.

Antoine took me on a tour of his company and showed me the different kinds of work they did. I met up with his son who worked with him as well as other employees whom I also knew from years before.

Around 5:30 we left, each in our own cars, and drove to the nearby city to catch up with Daniel. I would be leaving from there to go back home, as I had been gone for over a week.

We had a great dinner and an even greater conversation. We had not been together for over three years, so we had much catching up to do. They both had children, so a lot had transpired in their families. If memory serves, we spent over four hours together, talking about everything that came to mind. We actually had to leave because the restaurant was closing.

It was somewhat like old times. There I was with my two older brothers, laughing, crying, and sharing stories. One person was missing—our sister, Andrée—but we all agreed that she would be harder to bring back into the fold. Antoine shared with us that, though he had some communication with her and the occasional visit, it was not like it was before Mother passed away. As for Daniel, he had not talked to her since that unfortunate event back in 1996.

After a wonderful evening, we went our separate ways with the agreement that we would stay in touch and that the long separation was over. More tears…

Over the following couple of years, there were regular phone calls and several visits where either I went to see them or they came to see me.

Over time, Antoine and I became concerned about Daniel's behaviour and health. Daniel's illness and restricted mobility made him very depressed. One of his legs had been amputated because of his diabetes and he was more or less homebound. Antoine and I had a long conversation to determine what we could do to help.

It turned out that Antoine needed someone to do some online research for him. I had just replaced my computer, so I offered to have my old one refurbished to give to Daniel. I could then show him how to use it.

Antoine would give him research projects to work on. To help Daniel financially, Antoine would give him prepaid vouchers to buy food and other necessities as well as rental car vouchers, so he could travel to see his children who lived an hour or so away.

These new challenges—along with Antoine's financial generosity—gave Daniel a renewed will to live, energy, and a sense of pride at being able to contribute and do something meaningful. He had been given a new lease on life.

There still remained the issue of our sister, but none of us could come up with an approach with which we felt comfortable. Meanwhile, as time passed, the relationship among the three of us flourished.

In September 2001, you will remember the tragic events in New York City that changed all of our lives forever. Do you remember where you were and what you were doing when you found out and possibly saw first-hand the horrific carnage? I do, and it is something that I will never forget.

For several weeks, it took all my energy and willpower to get up and carry on with my life. Travelling by air became very stressful. My first planned air travel was a nightmare. At the airport gate, I could not even make myself get on the plane. Visions of what had transpired overpowered me and I cancelled my flight right there and then.

It took several weeks for me to talk myself down and get back to travelling again, although always with apprehension. In October, while driving home from a funeral, I was thinking of numerous things—the death of a good friend, the events of 9/11, and the issue with my sister. Somehow these were all connected in my mind. Life is short! I remembered listening to an interview with a well-known Canadian singer about the shortness of life.

"Yes, you can lose somebody overnight, yes, your whole life can be turned upside down. Life is short. It can come and go like a feather in the wind." – Shania Twain

Suddenly my eye caught a road sign. It was the name of the village where my sister lived. Without hesitation, I put on my signal and turned to go to my sister's home. There was no logical reason. It was purely emotional. I was going to show up on her doorstep as I had done two years before with my brother. We would either settle our differences or the end would be final. It was all or nothing.

I parked the car, walked up to the front door, and rang the bell. Though the inside door was open, the screen door was locked. I could hear the bell ring as I pushed the button several times. No answer! I looked around. They might be visiting neighbours. Not wanting to start going from house to house, I went back to my car, got a piece of paper and wrote: "Hi, was in the neighbourhood and stopped in to say hello. Jean-François." I stuck the note in the door handle and drove off, satisfied that I had started the process to communicate. The ball was in her court now. All I could do was wait and see.

A few days later, I received a call at work from my nephew, my sister's youngest son. His mother had called him to tell him of my note and that she wanted to talk to me and hopefully see me. I asked if this was going to be a good thing. His answer was clear… Yes! That evening was spent on reflecting on what I would say and do.

The next day I called her mid-morning. She was expecting my call. She explained that she and her spouse had been home when I had dropped by; however, her husband had been working in the basement with electrical tools and she had been drying her hair. Consequently, neither had heard the doorbell.

We chatted for a few minutes and agreed to meet the following Saturday morning. Due to my discomfort about how things would go, I asked if the two of us could meet at a coffee shop midway between where we each lived. She agreed. Leading up to the meeting day, I experienced a great deal of anxiety. Our last encounter had been very difficult and hurtful.

As agreed, we met at a coffee shop. I had a latte while she had a cup of tea. The meeting started off very subdued and low-key. Our conversation began with general topics—the weather, work, and the recent events of 9/11. She was curious to know why I had been in the area where she lived, given it was quite a way out of my way, so I explained that a friend had passed away and that I had attended the funeral that was held in the area.

We expanded our conversation to her family, then to our brothers and their families. I brought her up to speed on the latest information I knew. She wondered if I still lived in the house I had bought for Mother. I told her that I had stayed there for a year and then had sold it and moved into a small condo west of downtown that was closer to work and more appropriate for one person. She acknowledged that she was glad that I had stopped by and that we had the opportunity to talk on the phone and meet face-to-face.

Though there was no formal apology—not that I had even expected one—during our conversation she did say that the events during the reading of the will should not have happened as they did. That would be the closest to an apology I would get. We spent several hours catching up on what had transpired in our lives since that April day back in 1996.

She suggested that I come over for dinner in the near future. I thanked her for the invitation but told her that I would need to work on that possibility for a while. She full well knew that I had issues with her spouse because of some of his behaviour and things he had said to Mother on several occasions. I wondered if time really does eventually heal all wounds.

As we were getting ready to go our separate ways, she moved closer to me and gave me a hug and a kiss on the cheek. The healing process had begun two years earlier with my brothers and was now continuing with my sister. Would things between us ever be as they were? How would they be different? We would know with time.

"Indifference and neglect often do much more damage than outright dislike."– J.K. Rowling, *Harry Potter and the Order of the Phoenix*

In the fall of 2009, my brother Daniel passed away. He unfortunately had not really taken his own medical challenges seriously. He had been diagnosed with diabetes in 1980, the same year my father died but had not taken to heart what he needed to do to ensure his well-being.

He unknowingly became the role model I would not follow as I, contrary to my brother, continue to lead a relatively healthy life, maintaining healthy eating habits and maintaining an active life-style with lots of outdoor and indoor activities.

Eventually, in preparation for my retirement from corporate life, I bought a house in a rural area with lots of land where I cleared about 2 kilometers of trails in a beautiful forest that I could use at my leisure by walking around the meandering paths, snowshoeing or cross-country skiing all while benefiting from the beauty and the serenity of nature.

I also planned, designed and built a one-acre garden with over a dozen flowerbeds, a Zen meditation garden and a small vegetable garden that occupies part of my semi-retirement days.

Many changes have occurred and more will come as it pertains to the care of elders. The percentage of elders is increasing every year and the health system has to adapt to new demands and expectations. Caregivers are often people who come from outside the families because too often the families feel they are either too busy or are unaware of the existing support systems. It is often difficult for our aging parents to welcome these "strangers" into their lives; however, with patience and understanding, it is possible.

More precise and continuous information is required to sensitize families and elder people of the different possibilities that have become available; with more services and support to come I am sure.

Chapter 22
Epilogue

"Life is Short. There is no time to leave important words left unsaid." – Paulo Coelho

As I wrote the words that described the many life-changing events that make up our story, I am reminded that as we go through our individual lives, we encounter situations and events that can throw us off, if only for a few moments.

Life is short... so very short. When facing challenges, it is normal to feel hurt and to protect ourselves by building emotional walls around us.

Some individuals lose their composure and lash out at the situation and the people involved. Others shut down and sever all links or contacts. Either reaction can happen—sometimes both.

In these situations, try to minimize lashing out at others or shutting down completely. Take some time to reflect on what happened and consider your own part in it. Is there something you did that may have caused the situation? Is there something you could have done to minimize or even prevent the unfortunate turn of events? This reflection might take some time, sometimes too long. Don't let your ego control you.

Putting my thoughts to paper has taken me many years. The first few years were extremely difficult as all the past memories engulfed my mind. The grief and sadness of losing Mother were often too painful. I knew I wanted to tell my story as I felt that it would help me complete my journey. Also, I feel that too often, the grown children's knee-jerk reaction is to try and control or influence their parents to go live in a nursing home or care facility. Sometimes circumstances require such a decision but not always.

Many years after I cared for Mother and the subsequent rift with some of my family members, I came to the realization that people around us, be they friends, colleagues, or family members, do not and cannot be expected to see things as we do. It is easy to be blinded by our own past and our own experiences. We all come from different backgrounds and experiences. Though some actions and behaviours were a given for me, they necessarily were not for my brothers and sisters.

Back in 1982, I invited Mother to come and live with me, without really fully thinking it through. For me it was an obvious and logical choice. She had cared for all of us and especially for me when I was sick, so it was now my turn to care for her.

Mother spent ten years thinking about my invitation, about what it would mean to her and to me. What was missing from those ten years were early and regular conversations with siblings about mother's failing health and the possibility for her to move in with one of her children.

Over time, as I pondered over Mother actually moving in with me, coupled with my frequent invitation to do so, I should have engaged my siblings in a conversation about the option of Mother coming to live with me and why putting her in a nursing home was out of the question, at least until it was inevitable.

In hindsight, I can see what I could have done differently. Perhaps these suggestions as they pertain to supporting and caring for an elder parent can help others in similar situations:

- Start conversations early regarding the "what ifs" with siblings and parent(s). Before something happens, consider what the children would do about an unforeseen situation (e.g., issues involving health, finances, family dynamics, etc.) that might render a parent more vulnerable and dependent. These conversations should also include what the parent desires in case of death or terminal illness.

- Set out and agree upon some general principles and actions or reactions to ensure the well-being of the parent(s). This will ensure that there are no surprises and that no one is blind-sided. It also ensures that the wishes and desires of the parent(s) are respected.

- At least once a year, during a family gathering, make a point of revisiting these principles and actions to ensure pertinence and agreement by all concerned. Things may change and certain actions or principles may need to be adjusted to one or more individual's circumstances.

- Keep the lines of communication open at all times between parents and siblings, and among siblings.

Pertaining to the caregivers, I learned several lessons that you the potential future caregiver might want to consider:

- Make sure you do not minimize your own personal life, including your personal needs and expectations, i.e. hobbies, interests, travel, etc. nor your social life with existing friends or the development of other friendships going forward.

- Hiring an outside caregiver to supplement your involvement is quite acceptable given everyone leads very busy lives; however, that stranger is not a family member and it will be very difficult for the parent to accept and welcome such a person.

- Elderly people often refuse or decline help from family members or outside caregivers; however, from experience, when the benefits and the advantages of such support is explained, then acceptance is often easier. If appropriate and useful, highlight the challenges of not having someone nearby to help.

- Knowing Mother, we approached it from a perspective of what she would like to happen. After all, she had raised and cared for all her children all her life and now it was our turn to be there for her.

- Sometimes elderly parents refuse any type of support such as a cane, a MedicAlert™ bracelet, and a once-in-a-while caregiver who drops in, even some prepared meals in the freezer and refrigerator or other types of supports. In these cases, highlighting the benefits of having such support as well as talking about the potential dangers of not having such support mechanisms can be helpful.

To this day, many situations and encounters remind me of Mother. Whenever I see an elderly woman, whether I'm in a grocery store, walking on the sidewalk, going to a movie, or getting ready to board a bus, a train or an airplane, I am reminded of the wonderful time Mother and I spent together. If I determine that the woman in question is in need of some kind of assistance, then I offer it in any way I can. This is an example of how the nearly four years of living with and caring for Mother have had a lasting impact on me.

In my personal life, I have followed through on a quote from Grace Hopper throughout my career: "It's easier to ask forgiveness than it is to get permission."

Though I had encountered a lot of resistance and opposition in my journey of caring for Mother, I persevered, and to this day, have no regrets, only joy and wonderful memories.

Little did I realize that on that cold March day, when Mother touched my cheek, how her gentle and warm touch would have a profound and lasting effect on others and me. It would really be a "lasting touch".

Recipes

Resources

The following resources and organizations provide guidance and support for identifying and purchasing assistive devices in Canada or specific provinces. For readers living in other provinces or countries, I am confident that you will find similar organizations in your local community or online.

Search for assistive devices:

- Canadian Assistive Devices Association
  http://www.cadaonline.ca/

- Health Canada – Seniors and Aging
  http://www.hc-sc.gc.ca/index-eng.php

- Seniors Store – Products that make life easier http://www.seniorsstore.ca/

- Ontario Medical Supply
  http://www.oms.ca/products.aspx

- Search for mechanized staircase for reduced mobility
  http://www.acornstairlifts.ca

- Search for specialized bathtubs and showers
  http://www.premiercarebathing.com

Search for information on adapting and making your home more accessible to seniors:

- "Aging in Place" Information about services and programs available to seniors at Canada Mortgage and Housing Corporation. https://www.cmhc-schl.gc.ca/ or by calling one of the regional offices (Halifax, NS – Montréal, QC – Toronto, ON – Calgary, AB – Vancouver, BC. or at the National Office in Ottawa. Numbers are listed on the corporation's site at the above link.

- https://www.cmhc-schl.gc.ca/en/co/acho/index.cfm

Search for information on the different supports provided by local governments as well as private organizations in your region.

The Canadian Government and the Provinces
have support mechanism in place.

- http://www.seniors.gc.ca/eng/sb/ie/index.shtml
- http://www.servicecanada.gc.ca/eng/lifeevents/caregiver.shtml

Advocacy Groups

- http://www.carp.ca

- https://sprintseniorcare.org/home
- http://eldercarecanada.ca/links/
- http://www.advocacycentreelderly.org
- www.ccc-ccan.ca
- www.seniorszen.com
- www.lotsahelpinghands.com
- www.thefamilycaregiver.com
- www.caregiverstress.com

The global aging of populations, has led to many books and articles being written on the subject of caring of elderly parents. Check out your local library, bookstore or on the various websites of book providers.

"No matter what you've done for yourself or for humanity, if you can't look back on having given love and attention to your own family, what have you really accomplished?"

— LEE IACOCCA